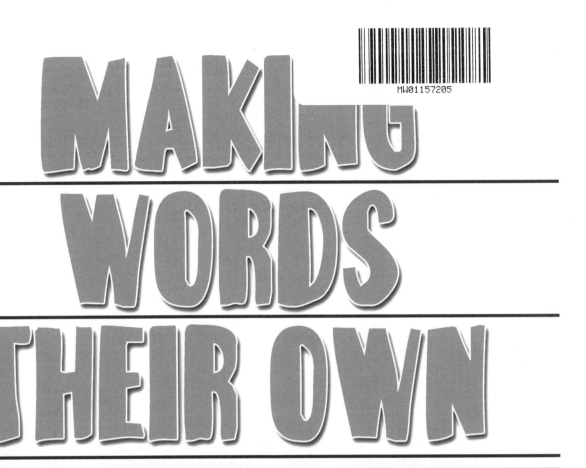

MAKING WORDS THEIR OWN

Building Foundations for Powerful Vocabularies

by Linda G. Allen and LeAnn Nickelsen

Crystal Springs
BOOKS

A division of SDE Staff Development for EDUCATORS

Peterborough, New Hampshire

Published by Crystal Springs Books
A division of Staff Development for Educators (SDE)
10 Sharon Road, PO Box 500
Peterborough, NH 03458
1-800-321-0401
www.crystalsprings.com
www.sde.com

Published 2008
Printed in the United States of America
12 11 10 09 08 1 2 3 4 5
ISBN 978-1-934026-16-8

Library of Congress Cataloging-in-Publication Data

Nickelsen, LeAnn.
  Making words their own : building foundations for powerful
vocabularies / by LeAnn Nickelsen and Linda G. Allen.
     p. cm.
  Includes bibliographical references.
  ISBN 978-1-934026-16-8
  1. Vocabulary--Study and teaching (Secondary)--United States. I.
Allen, Linda G., 1949- II. Title.

  LB1631.N53 2008
  428.1071'2--dc22

2008014080

Editor: Elaine Ambrose
Art Director, Designer: Soosen Dunholter
Production Coordinator: Deborah Fredericks

Ship & Anchor is reprinted with permission from Corwin Press. Jensen, Eric, and LeAnn Nickelsen.
Deeper Learning: 7 Powerful Strategies for In-Depth and Longer Lasting Learning. Thousand Oaks,
CA: Corwin Press, 2008.

Dedications

To my family—my husband, Larry; my sons, Ryan, Kyle, and Kevin; and my daughter, Lee—for their love, patience, and humor during this writing. I thank them for all the amazing words they have taught me in our lifetime together: unconditional love, understanding, confidence, laughter, honesty, curiosity, respect, compassion, serenity, enthusiasm, commitment, surprise, and, most of all, thankfulness.

—Linda Gilliland Allen

To my husband, Joel, who is the most positive, uplifting friend I know. Thank you for your support, for your incredible word choice contributions, and for being the best dad for our school-age twins, Keaton and Aubrey. Keaton and Aubrey, may you have a love for learning, a love for new and unique words, and a love for people. Thank you, Mom (Dolores Ann Heim) and Dad (Jim Heim), for encouraging me to be a teacher—it's the best profession!

—LeAnn Marie Nickelsen

Contents

Part Three: Vocabulary Strategies to Use After Learning

Teacher Resources

Acknowledgments

Special thanks to:

Dolores Ann Heim, a forever teacher, who added her microscopic version of "The Three Little Pigs" to our collection of strategies. Thank you, Mrs. H.

The students and teachers who have kindly submitted to testing, tweaking, and retrying the assessments and strategies in this collection. You are feisty and fun!

Lorraine Walker, for giving us this wonderful opportunity.

Barbara Jatkola, whose wisdom, experience, and impeccable judgment brought order to chaos.

Elaine Ambrose, whose sense of humor and say-it-another-way ability kept us searching for unique strategies and perfect words.

Introduction

There is no one "right" way to teach vocabulary. Different learners need different kinds of instruction, and not all words lend themselves to the same kind of teaching. But there are many effective strategies for teaching all kinds of words, and plenty of research that tells us how the brain learns words best.

This book is a teacher-tested and student-approved collection of powerful strategies for learning words. For students to make sense and meaning of new information, the research says they must process it in different ways at different times during the learning cycle. Therefore, we've organized these strategies into three groups—before, during, and after accessing new information whether through reading, mini-lessons, videos, Internet research, guest speakers, or hands-on projects. Students are all different, and teachers are, too, so you'll find that some strategies work just as well at other points in the learning cycle. When you find effective strategies that students love, you'll use them often!

We hope that having many ways to teach vocabulary together in one book will make your work a little easier. Students need lots of different pathways to own their learning, and these activities offer just that. We know your students will enjoy these strategies and the success they'll experience.

How to Use This Book

The strategies in part one, before learning, are designed to activate prior knowledge and stimulate memory recall and imagery systems. Use them to spark students' curiosity and motivate them to invest in the learning process, a sure bet for facilitating word retention. These strategies include preassessments to determine what your students already know so that you can design a unit that's appropriate, ways to preteach vocabulary, strategies for teaching structural and contextual analysis, and ideas for immersing students in rich language experiences.

The strategies in part two will help students to access new information as content is added during the learning cycle. Learners need effective ways to process additional layers of information, so this section includes metacognitive activities that encourage students to stop, think about new words, and self-assess. You'll find strategies for word comparison, context clues, and other ways to enhance students' thinking about new words.

Part three has strategies to use at the end of a unit to help students rehearse, analyze, and extend learning. With these strategies, students process information so that it enters long-term memory. This section includes strategies for word elaboration, meaning making, summarizing, reviewing, and higher-level word analysis.

Features of Each Strategy

Above each strategy title, you'll see **grouping suggestion**, **time allotment**, and **grade range**. These are based on our experiences, and since every class (and every teacher) is different, you'll want to adjust them for the needs of your class.

Each strategy starts with a **description**, followed by a brief explanation of **why it works** to improve vocabulary acquisition. You'll find information about how the brain takes learning into long-term memory or the latest vocabulary research. To learn more about cognitive research, refer to the bibliography (p. 141).

Materials and preparation are next. Designed for minimal preparation, most strategies use materials you have on hand, so you can use your time and energy teaching instead of preparing to teach.

Most strategies include **introducing the activity**, which shows how to teach students the new strategy with previously acquired content. This lets them focus on learning the strategy before they apply it to new concepts and words. This section includes the following components:

- Specific explanations and directions for students
- Opportunities to practice the activity with feedback
- Think-aloud language for modeling and questions for discussion.

Step-by-step instructions, also included in most lessons, guide students as they begin to apply a strategy to new learning. Use our examples or your own; no one knows your class the way you do. In this section, you'll find these components:

- A review of the steps so students ease into the practiced strategy with new content
- Wording to support modeling and think-aloud teaching
- Opportunities to practice the strategy with support and feedback.

Checking for understanding suggests ways to assess students' understanding and includes rubrics and checklists in many cases.

Ways to differentiate instruction offers ideas for modifying lessons for your community of diverse learners. You'll find suggestions for adapting lessons for multiple intelligences and different learning styles, as well as ways to scaffold instruction for at-risk students and meet the needs of students ready for a challenge.

Part One
Vocabulary Strategies to Use Before Learning

GROUPING SUGGESTION:
whole class

TIME ALLOTMENT:
10 minutes

GRADE RANGE:
4–12

ABC Brainstorm

There are several types of assessments. General preassessments give you an overall picture of where the class is in its understanding of a topic, unit, or concept. Preassessments of individual students gather definitive information on what each student knows and can do. Formative assessments during a course of study serve as checkpoints to see if instruction and learning are headed in the right direction, while summative assessments provide feedback at the end of a lesson or unit. ABC Brainstorm is a great preassessment, but it can also be used as a formative assessment when you want to know whether students' vocabularies in an area of study are becoming stronger.

Why It Works

ABC Brainstorm accomplishes two important goals. First, it gives students a global understanding of the types of words they associate with a topic. If they have wide background knowledge of the topic, you'll see that they've listed a variety of words related to the content. Students with little prior knowledge will have fewer words recorded on the organizer, and these will be more general.

The second goal is that it activates prior knowledge. When students process what they think they know about a topic, share the information, and debrief with the class, they bring to the frontal lobes of their brains information that will be the pegs for new learning. Do this activity two weeks prior to the start of a new unit, and students will be subconsciously making connections before you even start to teach content!

MATERIALS & PREPARATION

- ABC Brainstorm organizer (p. 17)
- Transparency

1. Make copies of ABC Brainstorm for students and a transparency for modeling.
2. Label the transparency "A Classroom" above the title.

Introducing the Activity

1. Explain to students that a preassessment helps teachers learn what students know or can do, so they can create interesting lessons tailored to the class. Assure students that although a preassessment may not be graded, they should do their best for it to have value.

2. Show students the ABC Brainstorm transparency and tell them that when they use the organizer, they will write words on as many of the letter lines as possible. They can skip around to record words, but in order to push their thinking across the alphabet, they should limit themselves at first to two words per line.

3. Tell students that together, you're going to do a practice ABC Brainstorm; the topic will be "A Classroom," as noted at the top of the transparency. Explain that you'll be the recorder and write words they call out when it's time. Tell them that a timekeeper will first give them 30 seconds of think time. When the timekeeper says "Go," they may start calling out words for you to write.

4. Choose a student timekeeper and tell her that when the activity begins, she'll say "Think," then she'll watch the clock for 30 seconds.

5. Say to students, "Our brainstorm is words associated with a classroom." The timekeeper says "Think." After 30 seconds, the timekeeper says "Go," and students begin calling out words for you to write on the transparency. List words on the corresponding letter lines as students call them out. Accept all words without commenting on whether they're appropriate to the brainstorming topic or not.

"A Classroom"
ABC Brainstorm

Name: _____

A	_____	**N**	_____
B	books, book bags	**O**	overhead projector
C	computers, calculator	**P**	paper, pens
D	desks	**Q**	questions
E	erasers, encyclopedias	**R**	rulers
F	fish tank, flag	**S**	students, scissors
G	glue	**T**	teacher, tables
H	_____	**U**	_____
I	independent reading	**V**	_____
J	jobs	**W**	windows, whiteboard
K	_____	**X**	_____
L	LCD projector	**Y**	_____
M	music, movement	**Z**	_____

6. When time is up, have a student read the words on the transparency and ask students, "What made you choose these particular words?" Some may say they looked around the room, and others may give different explanations.

7. Ask students, "If you look carefully at the words on the list, are there any particular ways they could be grouped?" Students should note that some words are school supplies, others are furniture, and still others are students' personal belongings. Additional categories could be technology, decorations, or plants.

8. Ask, "Could thinking in categories have helped you generate more words? When you have a time limit, would it be more difficult to list words by thinking of them in groups, or would it be easier?" Cognitive research shows that to store information efficiently, the brain looks for similarities based on certain patterns. When the learner needs to access those words, he can find them more easily because they are stored together.

Step-by-Step Instructions

1. Choose a unit of study you want to preassess. Wipe off the ABC Brainstorm transparency, place it on the overhead, and give each student a copy of the organizer.

2. Say, "You are going to spend 2 minutes searching through your memory to find words associated with a new unit of study we'll begin soon. I want to see what connections you already have stored in your brains about this topic. Some of you may know a lot about the topic because you've had courses or read about it. Maybe you've heard people discuss it. Or you may be only slightly familiar with the topic. That's fine, too." Remind students that you expect everyone to be at a different place in his understanding.

3. Tell students that you're adding one new direction to what they practiced earlier. "When I give you 30 seconds' think time, you

may not write your words on the front of the organizer, but you can use the back to jot down categories you could use to divide the topic. For example, when we brainstormed for 'A Classroom,' we could have listed furniture, students' stuff, and technology." Depending on your students, you may want to list topic categories on the board. The more often you model this part of the strategy, the better; students need lots of practice before they can do it independently. Say to students, "Determining the larger categories will help when you flip your paper over and start listing words on the front of the organizer."

4. Say, "Now flip your organizers over and jot down categories for our topic. Remember, first you'll have think time, when you can lay out your categories, then writing time. Our topic is 'Economics.' Ready? Think and organize your categories." Students might list categories such as expenditures, cost of living, unemployment, and government—terms they've studied since middle school.

5. After 30 seconds, say, "Turn your papers over and start listing your words." Stop students after 2 minutes and ask them to look over their organizers and circle any letter of the alphabet with a word next to it.

6. Since students always want to see what everyone else wrote, say, "Turn to your neighbor and share. If they've written a word that you think is awesome, add it to your paper, but don't circle the letter for that line. Later, when you do this again, you'll remember which words you listed independently the first time and be able to measure your progress as you learn more about the topic." Sharing their lists will further activate prior knowledge. When a student shares something she remembers about the topic, another student can have an "aha" moment, too. Sharing information helps students make connections—those pegs on which later learning will hang!

7. After a few minutes, bring the class together and talk about some of the words that came up when students shared with a partner. Ask, "How does that word relate to economics? How do you know that word?"

8. Following the whole-class discussion, collect students' organizers to assess their work, then use them as benchmarks to compare a second, similar assessment later in the unit. You can return them to students later to use for writing.

Checking for Understanding

Evaluate the organizers to get an idea of each student's background knowledge for the topic you will teach.

- If the student shows more than an average, grade-appropriate understanding of the core words for the content, administer a more specific preassessment to see if she needs an independent project to move beyond her knowledge base.

- For students who list few words related to the topic, prime their brains with basic information. Provide opportunities for watching videos; looking through print resources, including charts, photos, and diagrams; and handling artifacts. Preteach basic vocabulary for the unit as early as possible to build a stronger knowledge base.

Ways to Differentiate Instruction

- For students new to brainstorming, work as a whole class and call on volunteers to supply words.

- For English language learners, list the brainstormed words and new vocabulary on index cards with illustrations or mnemonics.

- For students who struggle with pacing, give extra time before the brainstorming to determine what the larger categories could be for the topic.

ABC Brainstorm

Name: _____

A _____	**N** _____
B _____	**O** _____
C _____	**P** _____
D _____	**Q** _____
E _____	**R** _____
F _____	**S** _____
G _____	**T** _____
H _____	**U** _____
I _____	**V** _____
J _____	**W** _____
K _____	**X** _____
L _____	**Y** _____
M _____	**Z** _____

GROUPING SUGGESTION:
whole class, then independent

TIME ALLOTMENT:
10–15 minutes per organizer

GRADE RANGE:
4–12

The Big Picture

Use this organizer to preteach all kinds of vocabulary. It's also great for reviewing words. The best part about it? The kids do the thinking and teaching!

Why It Works

When it comes to vocabulary, the brain wants to see the big picture—literally and figuratively. To teach new words, give students a memorable picture, symbol, or object to represent each one. This enhances their recall of the word's meaning. Better yet, invite students to create their own nonlinguistic representations of words. Attaching emotion to a word also makes it more memorable. When students make personal connections to words, they comprehend at a deeper level than if they just memorize definitions.

MATERIALS & PREPARATION

- The Big Picture organizer (p. 22)
- Transparency
- Small paper bag
- Colored vis-à-vis markers

1. Make copies of The Big Picture for students and a transparency for modeling.

2. Create a list of need-to-know words from a book students will read or a unit of study. For example, before beginning *Freedom Train*, we skimmed through the book and created a list of words that would be challenging for our average fifth graders. We included the page number where each word first appeared. List enough words so that each student has a

different one. If you have more words than students, ask for volunteers to take two words and two organizers.

3. Cut the list apart so that each word, with its page number, is on a separate strip of paper. Place these strips in the paper bag.

Introducing the Activity

1. Place The Big Picture transparency on the overhead.

2. Choose a strip from the bag, read the word aloud, and write it in the rectangle in the center of the transparency using a colored marker. Color enhances memory!

3. Demonstrate skimming the page where the word was found. You might say, "My strip has page 14 on it, so I'll look there to find the word *abolitionist*."

4. On the transparency, move to the box in the lower left-hand corner labeled "Word Context." Under "Word in context," write the page number, then copy the sentence that contains the word exactly as it appears in the book. Explain that you're including the page number in case other students want to know where the word is located.

5. Go to "Word Descriptions" and model looking up the word in a dictionary. In your own words, write the meaning in the box. If possible, include one or two synonyms. List the word's part of speech, based on how it's used in the sentence, and copy the pronunciation from the dictionary.

6. Go to "Word Connections" and explain that students have a choice here; they can write a simile, metaphor, or analogy; they can list more synonyms or related words; or they can use the word to describe a personal experience. Model doing this on the transparency.

7. Go to "Word Art" and, eliciting students' ideas, create a picture or symbol for the word that will help you and them remember it. Use color to enhance memory.

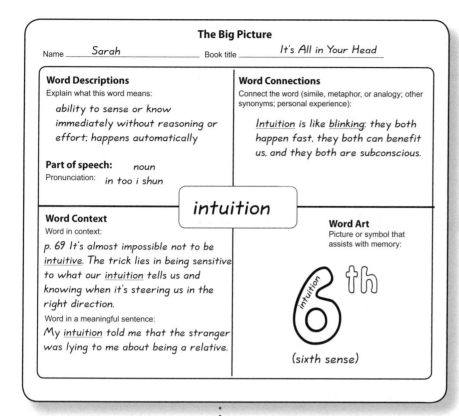

The Big Picture

Name ___Sarah___ Book title ___It's All in Your Head___

Word Descriptions

Explain what this word means:

ability to sense or know immediately without reasoning or effort; happens automatically

Part of speech: noun

Pronunciation: in too i shun

Word Connections

Connect the word (simile, metaphor, or analogy; other synonyms; personal experience):

Intuition is like blinking: they both happen fast, they both can benefit us, and they both are subconscious.

intuition

Word Context

Word in context:

p. 69 It's almost impossible not to be intuitive. The trick lies in being sensitive to what our intuition tells us and knowing when it's steering us in the right direction.

Word in a meaningful sentence:

My intuition told me that the stranger was lying to me about being a relative.

Word Art

Picture or symbol that assists with memory:

6th (sixth sense)

8. Return to "Word Context" and, under "Word in a meaningful sentence," create a sentence that connects the word to your life.

9. Explain to students that when they have completed their organizers, you'll collect and arrange them in order by chapter and page. The day before students are going to read a chapter, you'll give the organizers for that chapter back to their creators, who will take them home to practice how they'll present their words. The next day, each student will teach the components of her word. Since most adolescent brains can process no more than four chunks of information at a time, we recommend having only three or four presentations per class. Research shows that teaching too many words in quick succession hinders remembering any of them.

Step-by-Step Instructions

1. Give students copies of the organizer and have them draw strips of paper from the bag. Have them complete their organizers for their words, following your model.

2. Collect all the organizers and arrange them in order by chapter and page. The day before students will read a particular chapter, give the appropriate organizers back to their authors.

3. Explain that these students should come to the next class prepared to teach their words in a way that students will be most likely to remember them (dress up, bring artifacts, use voice changes or gestures, teach a mnemonic). They'll also use their completed organizers in their teaching. To model performing a word, you might act out the word *abolitionist*.

Make a sign from a piece of construction paper that has the international symbol for "no" and the word *slavery* (see illustration). Tape the sign to a ruler and use it as a prop.

4. On the assigned day, give each student 2 minutes to teach his word.

5. After the students have taught their words, display their organizers where everyone can refer to them for writing, review, and discussion.

Checking for Understanding

Use a checklist for assessment that includes the following:

- Completion of activity
- Accuracy in each box
- Creativity and color in "Word Art"
- Word descriptions that demonstrate understanding
- Creativity in choice of teaching strategy

Ways to Differentiate Instruction

- For a whole-class study of a challenging concept or word, create a large poster of the organizer. Add to it as students develop a deeper understanding of the concept.

- For students who love to draw, provide opportunities to represent words in cartoons, logos, and sketches. Share these with the class.

- Offer students who have a difficult time using a dictionary a word description that is an easy-to-understand, first-layer definition. This basic understanding will give at-risk students more confidence and provide a foundation for what is to come.

The Big Picture

Book title _____

Word Descriptions
Explain what this word means:

Part of speech:
Pronunciation:

Word Context
Word in context:

Word in a meaningful sentence:

Word Connections
Connect the word (simile, metaphor, or analogy; other synonyms; personal experience):

Word Art
Picture or symbol that assists with memory:

GROUPING SUGGESTION:
partners or groups for practice, then independent

TIME ALLOTMENT:
10–15 minutes

GRADE RANGE:
4–12

Caution! Synonyms Ahead!

Understanding the difference between connotation and denotation is difficult for many students. Sometimes it's evident that a student has used a thesaurus to find a "better" word, but that word doesn't really fit. It's important for students to understand the difference between the denotation (the literal meaning) and the connotation (the implied, emotional meaning) of words. In this strategy, students learn to analyze a word's meaning in a particular sentence. Do it before a writing assignment for added punch!

Why It Works

When students have a better understanding of the different ways in which words can be used, they'll have a greater chance of choosing the right words to say exactly what they mean. Every time you ask students to delve deeply into a word's meaning with this activity, hold them responsible for using the word correctly in their writing and speaking. After you have taught this lesson, use this activity again whenever you see or hear certain words misused in students' written and oral communication. Many students will need repeated experiences with connotation and denotation before they can master the concept.

- Caution! Synonyms Ahead! organizer (p. 28)
- 1 or 2 transparencies
- The Three Microscopic Pigs: A Thesaurus Disaster reproducible (p. 27)

1. Make copies of Caution! Synonyms Ahead! for students and a transparency for modeling.
2. Make copies or a transparency of The Three Microscopic Pigs: A Thesaurus Disaster.
3. Give each team a dictionary and a thesaurus.
4. Choose a common word that can be replaced with more specific synonyms (for example, *nice*, *trip*, or *good*) and create a sentence frame for it. If you choose the word *trip*, the sentence frame might look like this:

> The family was ready to leave for a
> _____ . *trip, jaunt, journey, expedition, safari, trek, excursion, outing, tour, voyage*

Notice that all of the italicized words would work in the sentence. This will help with brainstorming in the next section.

Introducing the Activity

1. Give each student a copy of The Three Microscopic Pigs: A Thesaurus Disaster or place the transparency on the overhead. Ask students which words are funny, awkward, or misused.

2. Discuss how using a thesaurus can enrich writing and speaking but how it can also be a disaster. Although the odd-sounding words in the story are synonyms, they can't be used as substitutes because they have slightly different meanings. Specifically, they have different connotations. For example, *mother* has a denotation of a female parent but a connotation of a loving, caring provider. **Stubborn** makes us think of **strong willed** and **pigheaded**, but **strong willed** can actually connote a positive character trait. It makes us think of someone who won't compromise her principles. In contrast, **pigheaded** describes a person who won't compromise or change her mind for any reason, no matter what. Connotations are all about the feelings that are tied up with words. Think of other examples together.

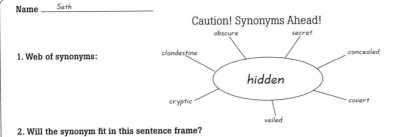

Name _____Seth_____

Caution! Synonyms Ahead!

1. Web of synonyms:

obscure   *secret*

clandestine   *concealed*

hidden

cryptic   *covert*

veiled

2. Will the synonym fit in this sentence frame?

We found a |hidden| passageway in the old house. _____

Synonym:	Does the word fit in the above sentence?	What critical attributes make it different from the target word?	Create an appropriate sentence for this word.
concealed	yes	———	———
cryptic	no	having a mysterious or ambiguous meaning	We couldn't understand the cryptic symbols.
clandestine	no	kept secret for evil or illicit purposes	The victim figured out the witch's clandestine act.
obscure	yes	———	———
veiled	no	not necessarily a real physical veil of material	Her veiled look concealed her true emotions.
covert	yes	———	———

3. Place the Caution! Synonyms Ahead! transparency on the overhead. Give each pair or group a copy of the organizer.

4. Walk students through the process of evaluating synonyms. In the oval on your transparency, write the word you chose in step 4 of Materials & Preparation (or use our example; see illustration) and have students copy it on their organizers. Then have the pairs or groups locate the word in the thesaurus and write four to seven synonyms extending from the oval to create a web.

5. Create a sentence frame for the word and write it on the transparency on the line under number 2. Have students copy your frame on their organizers. Box in the chosen word and model this on your transparency.

6. Ask students to share the synonyms they found. As a class, choose six synonyms for a denotation and connotation study. Choose words that most students might not be sure how to use.

7. Write these six words on the transparency in the first column under "Synonym." For each word, ask students to decide the following:

   - Does the word make sense in the sentence frame in number 2? Say the sentence aloud, substituting the word you wrote in column 1 for the boxed word in the sentence frame.

   - Does the word sound right in the sentence?

- Tell students, "If you said yes, write 'yes' in column 2. You can move to the next synonym you wrote in the first column. If you said no, write 'no' in column 2 and move to the next two columns."

8. If the answer to column 2 is no, have students find the word in the dictionary. Ask them how the synonym is different from the word they wrote in the oval. Have them list the critical attributes of the word in the third column.

9. Have students create a sentence that uses the synonym correctly and write this in the last column.

Checking for Understanding

Check students' work to make sure the words are used correctly. Then have them use their organizers for a piece of writing that uses each word—a story, spelling sentences, directions, poetry, or a news article. Evaluate whether each word is used correctly.

Ways to Differentiate Instruction

- For students who struggle with the difference between denotation and connotation, provide scaffolding with more examples and a chart with three columns labeled "Word," "Denotation," and "Connotation." List examples as your students brainstorm and find words in their reading—for example, *adequate* (word), *good enough* (denotation), *not the best* (connotation); *excuse* (word), *explanation* (denotation), *weak reason* (connotation).

- Invite students to write their own thesaurus disaster stories to share with the class.

- Using a chapter book with dialogue, have students list words used in place of *said* (for example, *mumbled*, *yelled*, *whispered*). Have them work in groups to create a few large charts to display. Remind students to refer to these whenever they are writing dialogue.

- Provide students with a list of neutral words and ask them to find two synonyms for each: one word with a positive connotation and another with a negative connotation. For example, for the neutral word *vehicle*, students might supply *auto* as a word with a positive connotation and *junker* or *jalopy* as a word with a negative connotation.

The Three Microscopic Pigs: A Thesaurus Disaster

by Dolores Ann Heim (LeAnn Nickelsen's mother)

In days gone by, three microscopic pigs existed with their matriarch pig in a minuscule abode. One day, the mother pig said, "Four of us can't exist in this house. It's much too infinitesimal. Decamp and devise your own dwellings!"

So the three microscopic pigs left their haven, determined to devise their own quarters.

The first microscopic pig raised his quarters of straw to save time for frolicking. The second microscopic pig raised his from tree limbs, so he could slumber. But the third microscopic pig was zealous and raised his quarters with blocks of clay.

Soon a beefy, rotten wolf came to the straw quarters, thwacked on the door, and said, "Microscopic pig, microscopic pig, allow me to draw nigh."

"No! No!" retorted the microscopic pig. "Not by the ringlets of my chinny-chin-chin."

The beefy, rotten wolf blustered and wheezed. He exhaled, collapsing the feeble straw quarters, and ingested the microscopic pig.

A while later, the beefy, rotten wolf came to the quarters made of limbs. He thwacked on the door and said, "Microscopic pig, microscopic pig, allow me to draw nigh."

"No! No!" retorted the microscopic pig. "Not by the ringlets of my chinny-chin-chin."

The beefy, rotten wolf blustered and wheezed. He exhaled, collapsing the limb quarters, and ingested the second microscopic pig.

The next day, the beefy, rotten wolf came to the quarters made of clay blocks. He blustered and wheezed, and blustered and wheezed some more, but he couldn't exhale hard enough to collapse the clay quarters.

"I'll get that microscopic pig," the wolf murmured. "I'll maneuver up the head of the quarters and descend by the chimney."

But the third microscopic pig placed a substantial saucepan over the inferno of the fireplace just below the chimney. Down came the beefy, rotten wolf and docked right into the saucepan. Soon the microscopic pig had beefy, rotten wolf for supper and lived jubilantly ever after for the duration of his life.

Name _____

Caution! Synonyms Ahead!

1. Web of synonyms:

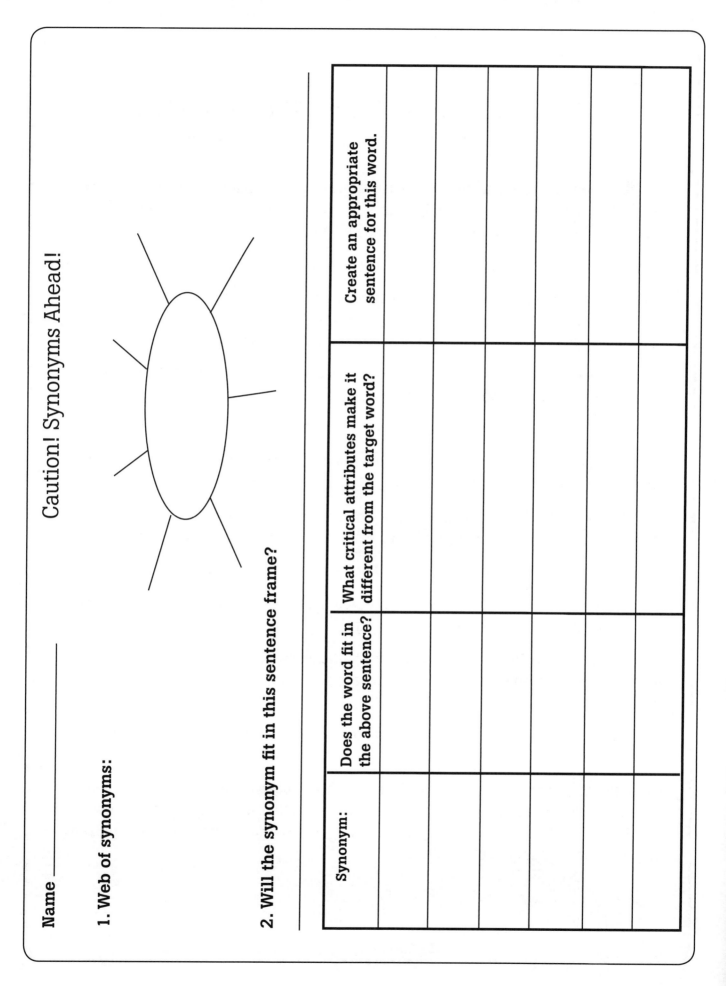

2. Will the synonym fit in this sentence frame?

Synonym:	Does the word fit in the above sentence?	What critical attributes make it different from the target word?	Create an appropriate sentence for this word.

Reproducible

Levels of Knowing

Levels of Knowing is a preassessment that allows students to evaluate the level of knowledge they have about specific words—whether they know the word well, have seen the word but are unsure of its meaning, or have never seen or heard it. This preassessment begins with the teacher selecting words that should be taught explicitly, or through context, or learned incidentally.

Why It Works

Levels of Knowing provides information to help guide instruction. Preassessment tells you which words need to be taught or retaught, which words need practice or elaboration, and which words students know. This allows for differentiation. Levels of Knowing helps students to evaluate their hunches about the meanings of words. This fast feedback is an excellent "priming the brain" activity.

MATERIALS & PREPARATION

- Levels of Knowing organizer (p. 32)

1. Make a Levels of Knowing transparency.
2. Choose six words that are important as benchmarks of understanding for the concept you'll be teaching. Write them on the transparency in the column titled "Words."
3. Make copies of the transparency for students.
4. Create a contextual sentence for each word you chose.

Introducing the Activity

Explain to students that you need to know which words they already know well in order to design upcoming lessons. Tell them that this preassessment will help them get ready for the new unit of study. Remind them to do their best on it.

Step-by-Step Instructions

1. Place the transparency on the overhead. Give each student a copy. Read the first word on your list and the contextual sentence you created for it. Repeat the sentence, then ask students to place their checkmarks in one of the three columns to the right of the word that describes how familiar they are with the word.

   * Wordmaster = I've seen this word often. I can define it and use it in writing and conversation.

   * Journeyman = I recognize the word, but I don't really own it yet.

   * Tenderfoot = I have no idea what the word means.

   Follow the same procedure for the rest of the words on your list.

2. Say to students, "If you checked 'Wordmaster' or 'Journeyman' for a word, write its meaning in the column labeled 'My Best Definition.' If you checked 'Tenderfoot,' define any part of the word, such as the root, prefix, or suffix, that you can."

3. Say, "Now look up the definitions of these words in the dictionary either independently or with a partner. Discuss the definitions and write them in the last column."

Levels of Knowing

Name **Delia**

Words	Wordmaster	Journeyman	Tenderfoot	My Best Definition	Actual Definition
lunar	✓			something to do with the moon	on the moon
phases		✓		times and seasons	parts of a cycle
craters	✓			deep pits on the moon	pits
eclipse			✓	I have no idea.	obscuring of one celestial body by another
tides		✓		something to do with waves in the ocean	rise and fall of the ocean's surface

* Wordmaster = I've seen this word often. I can define it and use it in writing and conversation.
* Journeyman = I recognize the word, but I don't really own it yet.
* Tenderfoot = I have no idea what the word means.

4. Collect the students' preassessments and use them to guide your instruction.

Tip

Preassessments strengthen instruction. Use them to:

- create differentiated lesson plans based on vocabulary knowledge
- determine which need-to-know words you will teach explicitly
- save instructional time by skipping words most students already know
- decide which words students can figure out from context clues
- create flexible groups to preteach or reteach words

Checking for Understanding

Students check their own understanding when they use dictionaries to evaluate their definitions. When they discuss definitions with other students, they refine their understanding of words and activate prior knowledge and connections to words.

Ways to Differentiate Instruction

- For students who already know the words you have chosen for assessment, allow them to select their own vocabulary words for the unit by scanning the text and related materials for challenging vocabulary.

- Pair struggling students with a mentor and provide dictionaries at the appropriate reading level.

Levels of Knowing

Name _____

Words	Wordmaster	Journeyman	Tenderfoot	My Best Definition	Actual Definition

* Wordmaster = I've seen this word often. I can define it and use it in writing and conversation.
* Journeyman = I recognize the word, but I don't really own it yet.
* Tenderfoot = I have no idea what the word means.

GROUPING SUGGESTION:
whole class, then independent

TIME ALLOTMENT:
15–20 minutes per organizer

GRADE RANGE:
4–10

Rootaffixionary

These collections of common roots and affixes are valuable resources that your students will want to keep. The jigsaw nature of the activity enables each student to become an expert on a particular root or affix, teach it to others, and collect roots and affixes in a booklet we call a Rootaffixionary. This strategy is appropriate before, during, and after lessons in a unit.

Why It Works

Examining the structure of a word can help students figure out its meaning. Many words are formed by combining affixes (prefixes and suffixes) and root words. Although there are relatively few affixes, they appear in a large number of words, so knowing the meanings of common affixes and roots helps students to quickly figure out a word's meaning, especially when the word appears in isolation without context clues.

MATERIALS & PREPARATION

- Small paper bag
- Rootaffixionary organizer (p. 38)
- Transparency

1. Decide whether you're going to teach roots, prefixes, or suffixes first. Let's say you choose prefixes. Select common prefixes your students are likely to come across or use in their reading, writing, and speaking. Have one prefix for each student. Write the prefixes on strips of paper and place them in the paper bag.

2. Make copies of the Rootaffixionary organizer for students and make a transparency to use for modeling. Each student will need a copy of the organizer for "Introducing the Activity," a copy to fill out for the prefix he draws, and a copy each time a student presents a word part.

3. Provide dictionaries, thesauruses, and other sources of roots, prefixes, and suffixes for students.

Affixes and Roots

* Common prefixes: *ab, ad, ap, at, bi, co, com, con, de, dis, em, en, ex, im, in, mono, ob, post, pre, pro, re, sub, super, trans, tri, un*

* Common suffixes: *al, ance, ancy, ble, ence, er, ful, ian, ic, ical, ist, ity, less, ly, ment, ness, or, ous, sion, tion, ward*

* Greek roots (begin with Greek roots because they're easier to locate in words): *aster, auto, bio, chlor, chron, derm, eco, geo, gram, graph, hydro, hyper, hypo, logo, meter, micro, mono, phil, phon, phos, photo, pol/polis, scope, tech, therm, zoo*

* Latin roots: *aud, bene, cred, dict, duct, fac, fact, fer, ject, jud, junct, mis, mit, mot, mov, par, pon, port, pos, spect, stat, tend, tens, ven, vent, vid, vis, voc, vor*

Introducing the Activity

1. Explain to students that discovering the meanings behind some words is a process similar to searching for clues in a riddle. The tips they're about to learn will help them figure out many words. They'll draw a slip of paper with a common prefix written on it from the bag. Each student will become a scholar on his prefix and will teach the class what he learns about it. Eventually, every student will be held accountable for learning all the prefixes, so each student will need to take notes on a copy of the Rootaffixionary organizer while the other students are teaching their prefixes. At the end of the presentations, each student will have a collection of all the prefixes taught. Students will use these all year for vocabulary and spelling instruction, writing, and part-to-whole learning.

2. Choose one prefix to model how to use the organizer. We've chosen the prefix *re* for our example.

3. Give each student a copy of the organizer and place the transparency on the overhead.

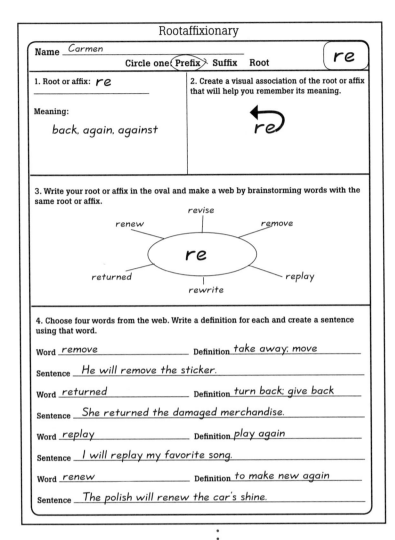

Rootaffixionary

Name _Carmen_

Circle one (Prefix) Suffix Root

re

1. Root or affix: _re_

_____

Meaning:

back, again, against

2. Create a visual association of the root or affix that will help you remember its meaning.

_re_

3. Write your root or affix in the oval and make a web by brainstorming words with the same root or affix.

revise

renew   _remove_

re

returned   _replay_

rewrite

4. Choose four words from the web. Write a definition for each and create a sentence using that word.

Word _remove_   Definition _take away; move_

Sentence _He will remove the sticker._

Word _returned_   Definition _turn back; give back_

Sentence _She returned the damaged merchandise._

Word _replay_   Definition _play again_

Sentence _I will replay my favorite song._

Word _renew_   Definition _to make new again_

Sentence _The polish will renew the car's shine._

4. Ask students to write **re** in the box in the upper right-hand corner of the organizer and on the line in box 1. Have them circle whether it is a prefix, a suffix, or a root. Tell students that **re** can mean "back, again, or against" and that the meanings of prefixes and suffixes can be found in a dictionary, just as the meanings of words can. Have them write those meanings below the line in the first box. Model this on the transparency.

5. Next ask students to create a visual representation to help them remember the meaning of the prefix **re** in box 2. This can be a sketch, a diagram, or whatever helps them to picture the meaning in their minds. Choose a student to draw her visual representation on the transparency.

6. In box 3, have students write **re** in the oval. Ask them to brainstorm words that begin with this prefix to create a web. Write their brainstormed words on the transparency, then have them copy this web on their organizers.

7. Ask students to choose four frequently used words from the web in box 3. Since you're modeling this, you might want to take a quick vote to get the four words. Have students write one word on each of the four "Word" lines in box 4.

8. Model how to locate the definition of one of the words in a dictionary. Then write the definition and a sentence using the word correctly on the transparency.

Step-by-Step Instructions

1. Now that students know how to complete the organizer, they're ready to do one independently. Give each student a clean copy of the organizer. Have each one draw a strip from the bag.

2. Have students complete their organizers, with help as needed, and prepare to present their findings to the class.

3. Have only two to four students teach their word parts each day so that other students remember the information. Distribute a clean copy of the organizer to each student for each presentation. While a student teaches, the rest of the class should be taking notes on the organizer. Remind students to make their presentations fun, lively, and creative. We recommend that students present their words in the following manner:

   Box 1: Report the meaning they've found to the class.

   Box 2: Draw their visual association on the board and encourage students to create their own symbols.

   Box 3: Report the words that they've found and invite the class to brainstorm other words.

   Box 4: Ask students to work independently or pair up to choose four words that have been discussed, then create their own sentences.

4. After all the students have presented their findings, have each student divide her completed organizers into three categories—roots, prefixes, and suffixes. Then have her arrange the organizers in each category alphabetically. The root or affix written in the upper right-hand corner of each organizer will make for easy alphabetizing. Ask the student to create a colorful title page for each section, then bind the organizers together into a booklet.

Tip

We recommend teaching each group of word parts—prefixes, suffixes, and roots—within a one-week period, so within three weeks, all the material is covered. We do prefixes first, suffixes second, and finally roots. When you're done, each student will have his own Rootaffixionary booklet to use as a resource throughout the school year.

Checking for Understanding

- Check students' organizers for completeness and accuracy.
- While each student is teaching his affix or root, assess his level of preparation and creativity, the accuracy of his information, and the quality of his presentation.
- Assess learning with periodic quizzes on prefixes, suffixes, and root words to determine whether students have learned the meanings of the affixes and roots they have been taught.
- Assess students' written work to notice whether they are using words with affixes correctly.

Ways to Differentiate Instruction

- For students who recognize isolated prefixes and suffixes but have trouble distinguishing them in a word, try "I Spy." Using a passage from any book, have students find words with prefixes and suffixes. If you make copies of the text, students can use a highlighter to circle them. Watch for students who mistake letters at the beginning of a word, such as *re* in *reason*, for a prefix.

- Recognizing patterns helps plant learning in long-term memory. Show students how knowing prefixes and suffixes can unlock the meanings of words. For example, the words *unprepared*, *unequal*, and *unpopular* have one thing in common: they are all opposites of the root word.

- For kinesthetic learners, create word tiles from paper or ceramic tile samples. Write a prefix, suffix, or root word on each tile. Give students time to build words and say them aloud to begin to train their ears and eyes to recognize correct combinations.

- Students new to English can work with a mentor. Provide a picture dictionary for them to use. Other students may need a simple dictionary to check a word's spelling. For example, the base word *write* could have *re* added to the beginning and *ing* added to the end. At some point, the student needs to learn that the *e* is dropped before the *ing* is added to create the word *rewriting*.

Rootaffixionary

Circle one: Prefix   Suffix   Root

1. Root or affix:
_____

Meaning:

2. Create a visual association of the root or affix that will help you remember its meaning.

3. Write your root or affix in the oval and make a web by brainstorming words with the same root or affix.

4. Choose four words from the web. Write a definition for each and create a sentence using that word.

Word _____ Definition_____

Sentence _____

Word _____ Definition_____

Sentence _____

Word _____ Definition_____

Sentence _____

Word _____ Definition_____

Sentence _____

GROUPING SUGGESTION:
whole class, then groups

TIME ALLOTMENT:
30 minutes

GRADE RANGE:
4–12

Semantic Passage Design

Semantic Passage Design requires students to use their prior knowledge of specific content or narrative words to predict how those words might be used in a text. After writing new sentences or a passage, students read the original text, taking in a new layer of information about the words. They then confirm or edit their writing as they deepen their understanding.

Why It Works

The more often students use new words, the faster they'll own them and be able to use them in their active vocabularies. This strategy encourages students to practice new words before, during, and after reading. It helps them focus on the key words and concepts in a unit of study, a book, or a narrative text and examine how they are used in the original passage.

MATERIALS & PREPARATION

- Semantic Passage Design Guidelines reproducible (p. 43)
- 2 transparencies

1. Make a transparency of Semantic Passage Design Guidelines.
2. Select a passage from literature or a content area text for students to read (from one of the students' books). Choose six to eight words from the passage that students need to know. Write

them on the transparency in the order in which they appear in the passage.

3. If students have no idea what a particular word means, create a word description.

4. If you have objects or artifacts to match the words, use them in your introduction to help build understanding.

Introducing the Activity

1. Explain to students that they are going to create passages or sentences using key words from another passage, then compare their writing with the original text to see if they used the words in similar ways. (For content area texts, especially for students who need scaffolding, allow them to write a stand-alone sentence for each word. This lets at-risk students concentrate on writing sentences that make sense without worrying about writing sentences that hang together.)

2. Remind students that the more often they use a word in context, the better the chances are that the word will be planted in their long-term memories.

3. Place the Semantic Passage Design Guidelines transparency on the overhead and ask one student to read the words aloud. Have students turn to a classmate and talk about the words. Give brief word descriptions as needed. (This isn't the time to fully teach the words, but do give quick descriptions that students can grasp.)

4. Review the guidelines on the transparency with the class.

5. For content area words, ask students to predict, based on the words listed, which content area they will be writing about—for example, science, social studies, or mathematics. This gives them a context for their writing. For words from literature, ask them to predict the genre.

6. Explain that you'll begin a passage using the listed words, but you'll need their help to continue it.

7. Look over the list of words as a class, then ask students to discuss them briefly in groups.

8. Write an introductory sentence on the remaining blank transparency. Ask students to brainstorm what could follow,

then invite one student to suggest the next sentence. Refer often to the Semantic Passage Design Guidelines transparency. Continue until all the words are used.

9. Reread the passage and discuss how the listed words are used.

10. Have students read the original passage that contains the listed words. Discuss whether the meanings in the passage you wrote together differ from those in the original passage.

Step-by-Step Instructions

1. Give students six to eight vocabulary words that appear in a passage from literature or a content area text.

2. Ask them to get into groups and talk about the definitions of the words. If any group would like a word explained, they can ask.

3. Review the Semantic Passage Design Guidelines transparency.

4. Ask students to predict the content area or genre the words are from. If they have difficulty, give them the answer so that they have a context for their writing.

5. Give students the option of writing a passage using all the words or a separate sentence for each word. For example, if the words included *thunderstorm*, *vapor*, and *energy*, the passage might begin, "*Thunderstorms* can form at a warm or a cold front. Water *vapor* condenses in the clouds. There is also electrical *energy* in a thunderstorm." Remind them that sentences with the pronouns *I*, *you*, and *me* usually won't work with content-related sentences. For example, "I like to see cirrus clouds in the sky" isn't acceptable, but "Cirrus clouds tell us that bad weather is on its way" would be a better choice.

6. When they've completed their writing, have students read the original text and compare how the author used the listed words with how they used them. This will generate discussion that will enhance the meanings of the words and help identify misconceptions from students' prior knowledge. If their sentences or passages need editing or

---

Semantic Passage Design
Guidelines

1. Words must be used in the order listed.
2. Once a word has been used, it may be used again in any order.
3. A passage needs a beginning, middle, and end. Write complete sentences.
4. The form of the words can be changed. For example, *instruct* can become *instruction, instructs,* or *instructed.*

1. meteorology	2. temperature
3. precipitation	4. radar
5. continent	6. weather station

The study of weather is called meteorology.
Meteorologists measure temperature, air
pressure, wind, and precipitation. They use many
tools to collect weather data and to track
storms. Radar is used to track storms as they
move across the continent. There are weather
stations all over the world to collect data and
help inform meteorologists about the weather.

modifying to revise incorrect information, give them time to do that now, so they aren't learning misinformation. It's easier to unlearn incorrect information sooner rather than later.

Checking for Understanding

As an evaluative activity, have the class discuss how the words were used in their own writing and in the original text. Did the original text extend their understanding of the words? Were the relationships between the vocabulary words and the concepts in the original text similar to or different from those in the students' writing? If you prefer a checklist of writing skills, consider these criteria for proficiency:

- Engaging introduction
- Organized ideas
- Logical sequencing
- Effective use of words or phrases to convey intended message

Ways to Differentiate Instruction

- For English language learners or at-risk students, review word meanings and help them make connections to their background knowledge before they begin to write.

- Have students who have difficulty with processing dictate their sentences to a scribe or work with a partner.
- Have on hand photos or illustrations that will help at-risk learners grasp concepts, especially for content area vocabulary.

Semantic Passage Design
Guidelines

1. Words must be used in the order listed.

2. Once a word has been used, it may be used again in any order.

3. A passage needs a beginning, middle, and end. Write complete sentences.

4. The form of the words can be changed. For example, *instruct* can become *instruction*, *instructs*, or *instructed*.

_____

_____

_____

_____

_____

_____

_____

_____

_____

_____

Ship & Anchor Connections

When you really want students to relate the new to the known, this is the strategy to use. Ship & Anchor Connections works best with the whole class. Use it to teach the meaning of a new word—the "ship"—by relating it to a commonly known word—the "anchor." When students have connected the new concept to an existing concept, the two words are compared and contrasted.

Why It Works

Cognitive theory research has shown that we learn best when we can relate a new concept to a known concept. We store new information based on how similar it is to what we already know. Research also indicates that comparing and contrasting is a powerful processing strategy—it enhances both memory and understanding.

MATERIALS & PREPARATION

- Ship & Anchor Connections organizer (p. 47)
- Transparency
- Large chart paper or poster board (optional)
- Vis-à-vis markers

1. Make a transparency of Ship & Anchor Connections or transfer it to large chart paper or poster board and laminate it.

2. Choose a vocabulary word from the content area you are studying or from a book students are going to read. Select a concept students must fully understand to comprehend the content area. For example, for a unit about amphibians, they'll need to understand the word *molt*. This is the "ship" word.

3. Choose a second word with a meaning similar to the new word. You want this "anchor" word to be one most of your students are likely to understand. For example, *shedding* has a meaning similar to *molt* but is likely to be more familiar to students.

Introducing the Activity

1. Place the transparency on the overhead or display the Ship & Anchor Connections poster if you made one. Explain that it shows how the brain learns new information. Tell students, "A ship will float away if it's not anchored. Learning new information is similar. A word or concept is likely to float away from our memory if we don't anchor it to something we already know."

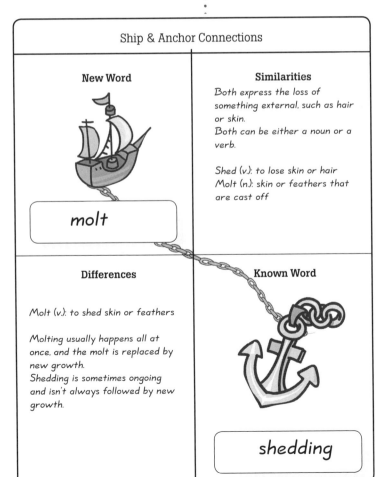

Ship & Anchor Connections

New Word

molt

Similarities

Both express the loss of something external, such as hair or skin.
Both can be either a noun or a verb.

Shed (v.): to lose skin or hair
Molt (n.): skin or feathers that are cast off

Differences

Molt (v.): to shed skin or feathers

Molting usually happens all at once, and the molt is replaced by new growth.
Shedding is sometimes ongoing and isn't always followed by new growth.

Known Word

shedding

2. Using a vis-à-vis marker, write the ship word you've selected in the box under the ship. Ask students to say it aloud and predict its meaning. Have a sentence ready that uses the word in context. Read it to students and ask them to predict the word's meaning again.

3. Give a description or definition of the ship word. Ask students to give you synonyms for it. Choose your anchor word from among these synonyms, or give clues so that students say your chosen word. Write the chosen word in the box under the anchor.

4. Give more elaborate explanations of both words as needed. List their similarities in the upper right-hand box, inviting students to help. They may use dictionaries, thesauruses, or other sources.

5. List the differences between the two words in the lower left-hand box. Now that the ship word has been connected to the anchor word, students are ready to explore it further through their reading, a structured lesson, a video, or discussion.

Checking for Understanding

Listen for an original description of the new word rather than a rote definition or one that sounds just like yours. You want students to understand the word and how it relates or connects to a similar, more familiar word.

Ways to Differentiate Instruction

- Divide students into groups, give them clean copies of the organizer, and have each group study a different pair of ship and anchor words. Have the members of each group work together to process meanings and complete their organizers. When they have finished, have a member from each group join another group. Give each new group member 2 to 3 minutes to present his ship and anchor words to the rest of the group. Continue this process until all the groups have been exposed to all the words. When the presentations are complete, everyone will be familiar with all the new words.

- Students who are ready for a challenge can create a simile, metaphor, or analogy that expresses their understanding of the words.

- For students who need lots of repetition to process new information, create study cards. On one side of each card, draw a ship and write the new word. On the other side, draw an anchor and write the known word and other related words.

Ship & Anchor Connections

New Word

Similarities

Differences

Known Word

What's My Line?

This takeoff on an old TV show gets students to examine what they know about historical figures based on prior knowledge, inference, legend, and even tall tales. In the original *What's My Line?* a panel of four people had to figure out the unusual career, hobby, or special characteristic of a mystery guest by asking yes-or-no questions. In this version, students recall descriptive words that fit what they know about the person (their prior knowledge) before they begin reading. Then, gathering information from a variety of resources, they describe the person with stronger and more accurate adjectives. This strategy continues during and after a unit as students refine their understanding and use new content to synthesize and analyze learning.

Why It Works

Students often use common descriptors that they've heard associated with a particular historical figure. For example, Abraham Lincoln is described as honest, but few students can give a reason to support why they believe that's true. They don't have enough information to know how that adjective relates to his life, how history shaped Lincoln's personality, and whether the descriptor is appropriate. This strategy encourages students to look critically at what they *think* they know, compare it to what they're reading and learning, and then restructure their prior knowledge to include more specific descriptors. They'll increase their understanding of descriptive vocabulary and find out the "line" on different historical figures.

- What's My Line? organizer (p. 53)
- Transparency
- Index cards (optional)
- Box for drawing cards (optional)
- Picture of George Washington (or other historical figure)
- Sticky notes

1. Make copies of What's My Line? for students and a transparency for modeling.

2. Choose a historical figure for modeling (we'll use George Washington) and gather resource materials about him or her. Resources should include books, Internet articles, photos and drawings, poetry, and any other resources you wish to use.

3. Make a list of people from your unit of study. If you will allow students to choose a person to study from the list, write the names on index cards and place the cards in the box.

Introducing the Activity

1. Show students the picture of Washington and ask them to identify him. Say, "Tell me what you know about George Washington." As they begin to share, you can preassess their knowledge. Do they know much about his presidency, his role in creating a new country, his military leadership, and other historical facts about him?

2. Place the transparency on the overhead and explain the meaning of the question "What's my line?" Tell students that together, they're going to find out more about Washington's "line" by examining descriptive words, exploring more information about him from different perspectives, and adding new descriptors based on what they learn.

3. Ask students to brainstorm words that most people use to describe Washington. As they share, write their words in the box on the left-hand side of the transparency. Explain that new words will be added and some may be replaced by better choices as they access more detailed information about Washington. High school students can also begin a discussion on perspective. How

would British soldiers have viewed George Washington? How would slaves have seen him? Would those views have changed how people described him?

4. Show students the resource materials you've gathered. Choose a book and model reading a passage about Washington aloud. In the box on the right-hand side of the transparency, write any new words you find to describe him.

5. Have students choose any resource material and begin scanning for information about Washington. They can use sticky notes to mark text that indicates or implies a character trait. After 10 minutes, ask students for any new information they have found and write additional descriptors in the box on the right side of the transparency. Ask students to compare the words on the right with those on the left and to consider whether each one on the left is still accurate. Words that students feel are still valid descriptors of Washington can be added to the list on the right. Students should refer to the text marked by sticky notes to support their opinions.

6. Refer students to the box at the bottom of the transparency and explain that this is where they'll record their comments and reflect on their understanding after they have added this new layer of learning. They should choose two or three adjectives from the right-hand list and include specific examples from text to support why they chose these words.

What's My Line?

Name _Rosario_

Historical Figure _George Washington_

When I think of
George Washington,
I think of these words:

- _truthful_
- _intelligent_
- _smart_
- _ragged_
- _starving_
- _____
- _____
- _____
- _____

After reading and studying, I would use these words to describe

George Washington

- _courageous_
- _confident_
- _ambitious_
- _angry_
- _heroic_
- _religious_
- _modest_
- _credible_
- _devoted_
- _intelligent_

My comments or reflections:

One word that I added to my list was modest. In the reading, I found a statement that supports this word: "I do not think myself equal to the command I am honored with."

Step-by-Step Instructions

1. Assign a person from your unit of study to each student or pair of students, or have each student or pair draw an index card from the box.

2. Give each student or pair a copy of the organizer.

3. Have students reflect on the characteristics of the person they are going to study. Have them identify 5 to 10 key words from their prior knowledge that they believe characterize this person and list them in the box on the left side of the organizer.

4. Have students look through resource materials about the person they are studying and use sticky notes to tag text that implies or describes attributes or characteristics.

5. Give students 10 minutes to create a second list of descriptive words that characterize the person. Have them list these words in the box on the right side of the organizer and then decide which words from the first list are accurate. Have them add those words in the box on the right. Ask them to consider each of the words they have listed in the box on the right and decide whether they accurately describe the person.

6. Have students complete the organizer by filling in the box at the bottom.

Checking for Understanding

- As an evaluative activity, have the whole class discuss how their understanding of each person changed as a result of their research.

- Assess students' work by examining each student's second list of words to determine whether she identified 5 to 10 descriptive words. Also note whether she wrote a comment or reflection that adequately summarized her new understanding based on her research.

Ways to Differentiate Instruction

- For students who are ready to see the bigger picture of what they are learning, have them reexamine a historical figure from different points of view. If the figure you chose to study was Abraham Lincoln, for example, you would ask students to look at the person from a different historical perspective. In the case of Lincoln, what would someone from the Democratic Party have thought of him? Someone from the Whig Party? How would a freed slave have seen Lincoln? A plantation owner in Georgia?

- Have at-risk readers work with stronger readers or with the teacher to brainstorm what they know about the character and to find more accurate adjectives. Also provide research materials at a lower reading level or use a text-reader software program.

- Emotions are a vital link to long-term memory. To help students make that link, choose a particular event or period in history, such as the age of discovery, the cold war, the civil rights movement, or the Vietnam War, and have them find descriptors that would fit people who lived through those times. What qualities would a person have needed to be involved in the race to reach the moon, for example?

What's My Line?

Name _____

Historical Figure_____

When I think of

_____,

I think of these words:

- _____
- _____
- _____
- _____
- _____
- _____
- _____
- _____
- _____
- _____

**After reading and studying,
I would use these words to describe**

_____

- _____
- _____
- _____
- _____
- _____
- _____
- _____
- _____
- _____

My comments or reflections:

Part Two

Vocabulary Strategies to Use During Learning

All Hands on Deck

Our students have amazing thoughts and ideas, but sometimes when explaining or writing about these thoughts and ideas, students may not describe them as clearly as they might. They may not have the right words for what they're trying to say. A student scientist who observes the results of an experiment or the properties of an object, event, plant, or animal may lack the vocabulary to explain effectively what she sees. Students need to build a repertoire of descriptive sensory words for interpreting new experiences. Use this strategy during a unit of study to help them build a more accurate and in-depth vocabulary. Students use an organizer to describe sensory and other attributes of an object so they can efficiently and effectively communicate their understanding and ideas.

Why It Works

Students need strategies for brainstorming more specific, descriptive vocabulary to replace commonly used words. They also need time to create lists of specific words that help describe sensory experiences. In this strategy, students visualize an object, idea, or concept guided by a hands-on template of the five senses to generate the best words to use for a true understanding of what they perceive.

MATERIALS & PREPARATION

- All Hands on Deck organizer (p. 61)
- 2 transparencies
- Swatches of fabric varying in texture, size, shape, and color

1. Make copies of All Hands on Deck for students and a transparency for modeling.
2. Make a list of five to seven need-to-know words or phrases from a content area. Make copies of the list for students.

Introducing the Activity

1. Say to students, "When we want to describe something and we don't have it in our hands, we must visualize it or see it in our minds. Once we have a mental picture, how do we go about describing it?" As students share their strategies, write on the remaining blank transparency the different categories of words they use to describe something. These will include shape, color, texture, and size.

2. Review the list and say, "This will help to remind us of the different ways we can describe something." Then place the All Hands on Deck transparency on the overhead and discuss the five senses— taste, touch, hearing, sight, and smell—we use to perceive objects, people, and places. Tell students that they will use this organizer to describe fabric, then give one swatch to each group.

3. Give students time to examine the swatches using their five senses. Stop after each sense and have them brainstorm in their groups words and ideas, then list some of these on the transparency. Remind them that because each group has a different swatch, responses may differ. Here are some words and ideas they may generate:

   - **Taste:** not appropriate for this task
   - **Touch:** smooth, rough, soft, satiny, scratchy
   - **Hearing:** nylon jackets or corduroy pants that make noise
   - **Sight:** colors and words to describe patterns and designs
   - **Smell:** cloth may have a fresh, clean scent; cotton and wool have distinctive smells; dry-cleaned fabric may have a chemical smell

4. Make a fist and remind students that they can also use comparative size and weight as a way to describe something. Ask questions—"Is your piece of fabric about the size of a playing card? Does it weigh more than a slice of bread? Is it larger than a shoe box?"—to generate a discussion about using relative size and weight to describe something.

5. Open your fist, wiggle your fingers, and say, "What function does this item serve? What can you do with it?" Students may give answers such as these:

    - Fabric is used to make clothing.

    - Fabric is used for tents and sleeping bags to protect campers from bad weather.

    - Fabric is used for parachutes, towels, sheets, curtains, and even bandages.

    Add a few key words such as **clothing**, **tents**, and **sheets** in the palm of the hand on the transparency.

6. Make a motion of picking things up. This is the function connection. The kinesthetic motion will help cement in students' minds that an object is associated with the five senses, relative size and weight, and function. Say, "Looking at all these characteristics, in what category or categories does fabric fit?" Responses may include the following:

    - Manufactured products (e.g., furniture, rugs, toys, linens)

    - Clothing

    - Decoration

    Add these to the palm on the transparency.

7. Explain that the sensory word lists students have started will help them when they write.

Step-by-Step Instructions

1. Have students choose partners and give each pair a copy of the organizer and a copy of the list of need-to-know words or phrases that you have created. Ask each pair to choose

one word or phrase and write it at the top of the organizer. An example of a concept for social studies might be "Human actions modify the physical environment." Need-to-know words or phrases might include *neighborhood developments*, *industry*, *parks*, *urban offices*, *factories*, and *shopping complexes*.

2. Remind students that their perceptions of the word or phrase they've chosen might differ from someone else's, so when they visualize it, they need to think of details. What part(s) of the description will be the same as another person's? What part(s) might vary?

3. Have students go through each of the senses. Tell them that as they brainstorm descriptive words or phrases, they should list these in the corresponding boxes on the organizer.

4. Have students decide on the size and function of the object and possible categories in which it could fit, then write these on the corresponding lines on the organizer.

5. After students complete their organizers, have each pair exchange organizers with another pair. Ask each partner to use the other pair's organizer to create a drawing to represent the new word or phrase. The more specific and descriptive the organizer, the easier it will be for students to draw detailed pictures.

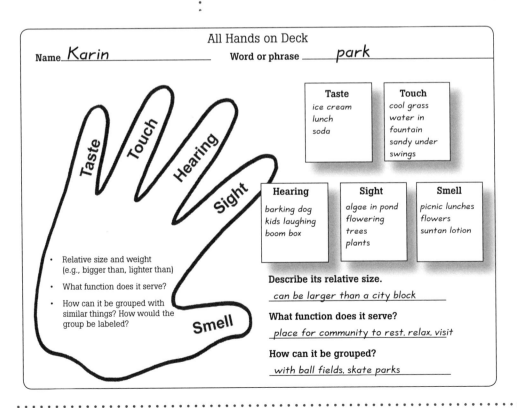

All Hands on Deck

Name __Karin__   Word or phrase __park__

Taste — Touch — Hearing — Sight

Taste
ice cream
lunch
soda

Touch
cool grass
water in fountain
sandy under swings

Hearing
barking dog
kids laughing
boom box

Sight
algae in pond
flowering trees
plants

Smell
picnic lunches
flowers
suntan lotion

Smell

- Relative size and weight (e.g., bigger than, lighter than)
- What function does it serve?
- How can it be grouped with similar things? How would the group be labeled?

Describe its relative size.
can be larger than a city block

What function does it serve?
place for community to rest, relax, visit

How can it be grouped?
with ball fields, skate parks

Checking for Understanding

Use the following criteria to evaluate students' work:

- Effective choice of words and phrases that convey intended ideas
- Age- and subject-appropriate language used
- Consideration given to all elements of the organizer
- Attention to details of another team's organizer for illustration

Ways to Differentiate Instruction

- For students who struggle with the language or have little prior knowledge in specific content areas, offer multiple experiences that connect descriptive words with sensory events. Use realia, photos, and artifacts whenever possible to provide background experiences and build understanding before a unit begins.

- Scaffold instruction by assigning words or phrases that are easy to describe to at-risk students. If necessary, work with them in a small group to complete the organizer.

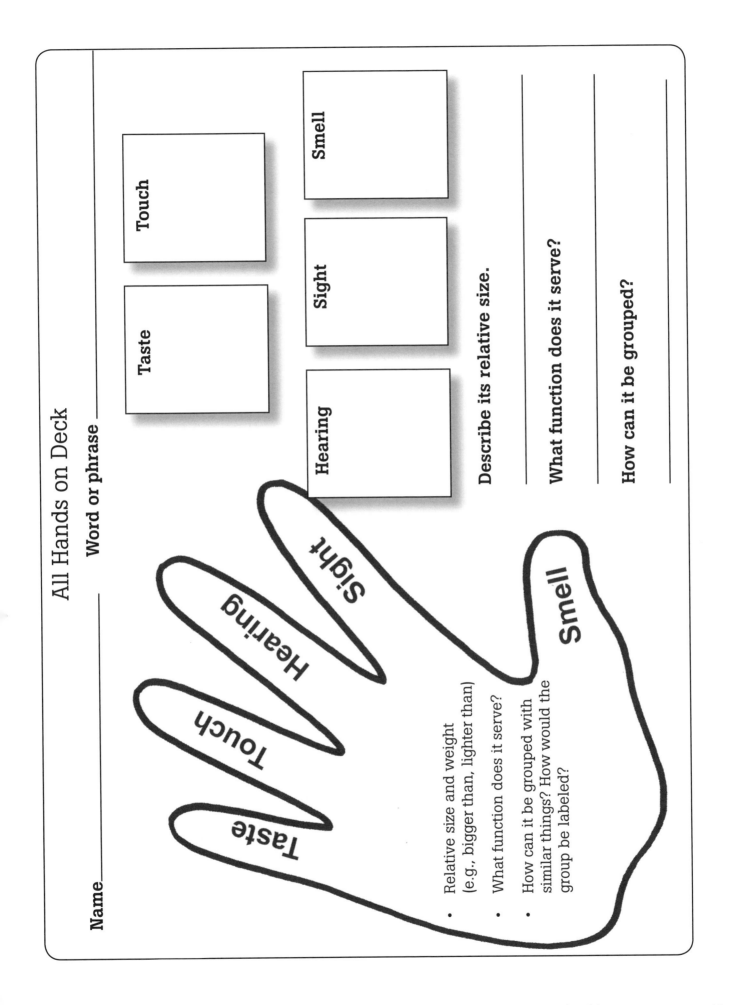

All Hands on Deck

Name _____

Word or phrase _____

Touch

Taste

Smell

Sight

Hearing

Describe its relative size. _____

What function does it serve? _____

How can it be grouped? _____

Sight

Hearing

Touch

Taste

Smell

- Relative size and weight (e.g., bigger than, lighter than)
- What function does it serve?
- How can it be grouped with similar things? How would the group be labeled?

GROUPING SUGGESTION:
partners

TIME ALLOTMENT:
10–15 minutes

GRADE RANGE:
4–12

Collecting Context Clues

When we ask students to watch for context clues in order to figure out unfamiliar words, many of them don't know what they are looking for. The Kinds of Context Clues bookmark describes common context clues students will encounter in their reading. Being familiar with the clues may help students figure out a word's meaning. Although students will use this strategy independently in their reading, we've included it here because it is so critical to comprehension that you'll want to review it with your class before they read any new text.

Why It Works

As adult readers, we've learned to read strategically, including automatically scanning for context clues whenever we see an unfamiliar word. We seldom stop to use the dictionary because we have other strategies to support us, although we may not consciously think about them. When students stop reading frequently because they've encountered an unfamiliar word, their comprehension suffers. Using context clues is a strategy that must be taught explicitly. When students master this skill, you'll find that their comprehension improves. Best of all, this skill carries over to all of their reading.

- Kinds of Context Clues bookmark reproducible (p. 67)
- Use the Clues organizer (p. 68)
- Transparency
- Books for students that feature a variety of context clues
- Highlighters (optional)

1. Make copies of the Kinds of Context Clues bookmark for students. If you can reproduce these on heavier stock and laminate them, they will last longer. Also make copies of Use the Clues for students and a transparency for modeling. Make enough copies of the organizer so that you have extras for students who find more than four unfamiliar words.

2. Read the books you will be using and choose several key vocabulary words not defined by context clues and other vocabulary words that the context helps to define. Look for examples of each kind of clue shown on the bookmark. You can also use the examples on the reproducible bookmark.

Introducing the Activity

1. Explain to students what you do when you come across an unfamiliar word: you look for clues so that you don't have to stop to look up the word in a dictionary. Ask students what they do.

2. Give each student a copy of the bookmark.

3. Say, "Context clues save you time and help you figure out the meanings of unfamiliar words when you're reading. There are several types of these clues." Go through the types of context clues on the bookmark, having students follow along. Here's what works for us.

   - Say the type of context clue, set in boldface italic on the bookmark. Have students repeat it and point to it on the bookmark. You can have students highlight each type if you want.

   - Read aloud the example on the bookmark or show students an actual example from a book. The unfamiliar word is set in boldface on the bookmark, and the clue is set in italic. It's a plus when students recognize the text you are using for an example, so be sure to scan their favorites for your examples.

4. Explain to students that they will practice finding these types of clues. Depending on grade level, you may want to divide this lesson and present it over several days so that students can focus on just a few types of clues at a time. Then, as a cumulative lesson, they could be responsible for all of them.

Tip

Reading is an invisible process. Students can't see what the teacher is doing inside his head to ferret out meaning. So teachers need to do think-alouds and let students hear how we are interacting with the text in our minds. They must hear us talk our way through each step before they can do this on their own. Invite students to listen in on your "mind" conversations as you introduce this strategy. Thinking aloud is a best practice—use it frequently and students will begin to internalize these skills.

Step-by-Step Instructions

1. Give each student a copy of the organizer. Have students choose a partner, then give each student or each pair the book you want them to read.

2. Explain to students that they will work with a partner to complete the organizer. Ask them to choose a portion of the book to read. Say, "You'll read through the chosen text with your partner as you normally would, but when you come across an unfamiliar word, write it on your organizer in the first column. Continue to read and look for clues around this word to help you understand its meaning. Use the Kinds of Context Clues bookmark to remind you what to look for. If the word is described or explained by a context clue, write the number of the clue and its key words in the column labeled 'Kind of Context Clue.'" Remind students that partners may come up with different unfamiliar words and will complete their own organizers. That's fine. By working with a partner, students can help each other to understand and find context clues and complete their own organizers.

		Use the Clues		

Name _Dylan_

Unfamiliar Word	Kind of Context Clue	Guess the Meaning	Actual Meaning	+ or −
humus	#3: "called"	decayed matter	decayed remains of plant and animal matter in soil	+
weathering	#6: root word	when rain, snow, ice, and wind break down rocks	action of weather conditions in altering the texture or form of exposed objects	+

3. Say, "Next, guess the meaning of the unfamiliar word and write your guess in the column labeled 'Guess the Meaning.' Then verify the meaning by looking up the word in a dictionary. Write a brief definition in the column labeled 'Actual Meaning.'"

4. Tell students to use the last column to write a plus sign (+) if their prediction was close to the real meaning of the word or a minus sign (−) if they didn't come close.

5. Remind students that this process will help them to see how context clues can explain the meanings of words. Stress that efficient readers use these clues to figure out meanings rather than stopping to search in the dictionary.

6. Have students continue this process until they complete the chosen text. Tell them to request another copy of the organizer if they fill the one they have.

7. When everyone has finished, discuss as a class which types of clues were more prevalent and whether some types of clues were not found at all.

Checking for Understanding

* Ask students to write a paragraph explaining what they should do when they come to an unfamiliar word. Responses should include the following:

  * Stop at the unfamiliar word.
  * Reread the sentence with the unfamiliar word to look for clues.
  * Look before and after the sentence for one of the eight types of context clues.

* Have students describe two or three types of context clues and explain why using context clues is important.

Ways to Differentiate Instruction

- For students who need more help identifying and using context clues, make copies of sample text at their instructional levels and highlight the context clues. Work with them in a group until they can recognize and use context clues to understand the meanings of unfamiliar words on their own.

- If pacing is a concern, teach the kinds of clues over several lessons. Review each type and reteach as needed before you introduce a new kind of context clue.

- Have students write context clues using words that they already understand. Direct them to create sentences that would help an English language learner to understand each word through the use of context clues.

Kinds of Context Clues

1. A **word after** an unfamiliar word: **Arachnids**, or *spiders*, have eight legs.

2. A **phrase after a comma**: Since I'm **tone-deaf**, and I *can't hear differences in pitch*, I'd rather dance than sing.

3. The word **called** before an unfamiliar word: *Animals without backbones* are called **invertebrates**.

4. Part of a **preceding sentence**: Children *love to talk*. They can be quite **loquacious**.

5. Part of a **following sentence**: The boys were **flummoxed**. Getting out of the woods was *confusing and bewildering*.

6. A **root**, **prefix**, **or suffix**: This is an **international** crisis. (*Nation* is the root, *inter* means "between," and *al* means "pertaining to." Maybe *international* means "pertaining to things between nations.")

7. **Comparison** or **contrast** words: *Unlike* her *shy*, *quiet* sister, Kayla is **boisterous**.

8. The **part of speech**: The sneaky kitty **slunk** around the barn, looking for the mouse. (Is *slunk* used as a noun, verb, or modifier?)

Kinds of Context Clues

1. A **word after** an unfamiliar word: **Arachnids**, or *spiders*, have eight legs.

2. A **phrase after a comma**: Since I'm **tone-deaf**, and I *can't hear differences in pitch*, I'd rather dance than sing.

3. The word **called** before an unfamiliar word: *Animals without backbones* are called **invertebrates**.

4. Part of a **preceding sentence**: Children *love to talk*. They can be quite **loquacious**.

5. Part of a **following sentence**: The boys were **flummoxed**. Getting out of the woods was *confusing and bewildering*.

6. A **root**, **prefix**, **or suffix**: This is an **international** crisis. (*Nation* is the root, *inter* means "between," and *al* means "pertaining to." Maybe *international* means "pertaining to things between nations.")

7. **Comparison** or **contrast** words: *Unlike* her *shy*, *quiet* sister, Kayla is **boisterous**.

8. The **part of speech**: The sneaky kitty **slunk** around the barn, looking for the mouse. (Is *slunk* used as a noun, verb, or modifier?)

Name _____

Use the Clues _____

Unfamiliar Word	Kind of Context Clue	Guess the Meaning	Actual Meaning	+ or –

Reproducible

Flag It & Tag It

Students must develop the ability to recognize when they know something and when they don't. This happens over time with practice in self-assessment. Flag It & Tag It is a strategy that focuses on this critical aspect of metacognition. It gives students a process for thinking about whether they understand what they are reading. One of the best parts of this strategy is the conversation that develops when students share their tags.

Why It Works

Metacognition is a higher-level thinking skill that can be taught as explicitly as how to decode sounds in a word. It helps students develop self-questioning skills as they are reading, and it supports the comprehension process when we teach students why they need different strategies. Flag It & Tag It teaches students to record what they're thinking, as soon as the thought occurs. This process encourages students to focus on and share what was going on in their minds, and their documented thoughts lead to robust discussions.

MATERIALS & PREPARATION

- 3 x 3-inch sticky notes, enough for each student to get 6–8

1. Give each student three or four sticky notes.
2. Choose two or three Flag It & Tag It symbols (see box) based on your lesson objectives, the difficulty of the text, and the students' instructional levels.
3. Make sure each student has a book at her instructional level.

Flag It & Tag It Symbols

W = Wow word; I like this word (Explain why you like it.)

? = Don't know what this word means (Guess its meaning, look for context clues, or look it up. Write its meaning.)

⛓ = Personal connection with this word (How is this word connected to your life?)

★ = Important word to know (Explain why you think it's important.)

CC = Context clue (Record the clue to the word's meaning.)

FL = Figurative language (Record the phrase; identify the type of figurative language, idiom, metaphor, or simile; and suggest a phrase to replace the original.)

Introducing the Activity

1. Explain to students that metacognition is a process of thinking about our thinking. Tell them that taking the time to visualize their thoughts will give them the reflection time necessary to start the comprehension process.

2. Explain that they will use sticky notes to document their thinking at various points during the reading. These notes will cue them when they are ready for a class discussion.

3. Write the symbols that they will use for this activity on the board. Explain to students that during their reading, they will use the same symbols on their sticky notes.

4. Model how to use the symbols and sticky notes, letting students hear your thought processes as you read and choose a word to comment on. Read a page from a favorite book. Stop when you come to a word that you consider a "wow" word. Let's say the word is *rambunctious*. At the end of the sentence, look up as if you are talking to yourself and say, "Wow, I really like the word *rambunctious*. I'm going to flag and tag that word." Take a sticky note and write the page number and a W at the top of it.

Then write the word *rambunctious* on the note. Keep thinking aloud; if you chunk words into parts to spell them, let kids hear that process as well. Explain why you like the word you've chosen. Say something like, "This word really shows the character being loud and rowdy. I even like the way the word sounds when I say it out loud." Show students your sticky note and explain that you'll tag the word *rambunctious* by attaching the note to the page where you found it.

Step-by-Step Instructions

1. Review the symbols on the board, hand out sticky notes, and assign the texts to be read.

2. Have students read their books and flag and tag the text as they are reading.

3. After 10 to 15 minutes, have them work with a partner to share their sticky notes. Many times, partners will have chosen the same words. This is a great strategy for activating students' prior knowledge as they discuss the words.

4. Debrief with the class. For example, you might say, "Did you think this particular choice of figurative language was helpful in understanding the character?" or "Did you find any context clues that helped you understand a word's meaning? If so, explain how you discovered the meaning."

5. At the end of the class, ask each student to attach her sticky notes to a sheet of paper with her name on it, then collect these sheets for assessment. Tell students, "I can't wait to see what was on your minds while you were reading!"

Checking for Understanding

- Observe students while they read silently. Take anecdotal notes regarding their use of the strategy.
- Listen to students' discussions as they share. Do they understand the symbols? Are their word choices valid ones? Are they thinking about their thinking?
- Assess their sticky notes for completeness, understanding, and accuracy.

Ways to Differentiate Instruction

- To ease struggling students into this strategy, make copies of the text to be read and let them mark words in the text using highlighters and symbols. Have them conference with you or a partner rather than documenting their thoughts on paper.

- Invite creative students to design their own symbols and a key.
- For students who feel overwhelmed by too many symbols, teach and practice one symbol a day until they show mastery. "Wow" words are good ones to start with.

GROUPING SUGGESTION:
whole class, partners

TIME ALLOTMENT:
8–10 minutes per word

GRADE RANGE:
6–12

IDEA Vocabulary Log

IDEA is an acronym for illustrate, describe, elaborate on, and associate the word. Many teachers like systems for teaching words explicitly, and IDEA was created specifically for that purpose. It's a way to organize the teaching of a new word. You'll want to use it before lessons or reading assignments, afterward for a handy review, and later for unit vocabulary tests.

Why It Works

Each component of IDEA is designed to help students use and remember a new word. To own a word, students should be able to connect the word to something already known, comprehend the word during reading, and use the word correctly in writing and conversation. IDEA is a way for students to achieve all three goals. Illustrating and describing the word help students understand it during reading, while elaborating on the word or creating a sentence for it assists in written and oral communication. Association helps plant new learning in long-term memory. Collecting all of this information about a word in one organizer makes it easy for students to review words for tests and access them when they're writing.

MATERIALS & PREPARATION

- IDEA for Vocabulary Words organizer (p. 78)
- Transparency
- Three-ring binder with dividers for each student
- IDEA Vocabulary Log cover sheet reproducible (p. 79)
- Colored pencils or markers (optional)

1. Make several copies of IDEA for Vocabulary Words for each student and a transparency for modeling.

2. Fold a sheet of paper to make three columns and label the columns "Need to Know," "Nice to Know," and "Where to Go." Need-to-know words must be taught explicitly for content mastery, nice-to-know words are those that students will learn incidentally through reading, and where-to-go words are those that students will locate in a dictionary when the need arises.

3. Decide which key words from a unit fall into each of these categories. The following questions can help you choose the words:

   - Which ones are most critical to understanding the content?
   - Which words do my students probably know already?
   - Which words are used most frequently in the text?
   - Which ones are important for building understanding for the next layer of learning?

   The words that are in the need-to-know column are the ones you will teach explicitly.

4. Create a Vocabulary Log notebook for each student using a three-ring binder with dividers.

   - Place several copies of the organizer in each binder.
   - Make copies of the Vocabulary Log cover sheet and place one in the front of each binder.
   - Leave the dividers in the binders. Students can use them to divide different content areas and to separate organizers for other word-learning techniques that they include in the binders. See, for example, Caution! Synonyms Ahead! (p. 23) and Vocabulary Bookmark (p. 91). They can also add a list of commonly misspelled words or their personal list of spelling demons.

Introducing the Activity

1. Explain that before students read a book or begin a study of new content, they need a clear understanding of several words. Hand out the binders and have each one write his name, class, and the date on the Vocabulary Log cover sheet. Then ask students to write the subject and date at the top of the first IDEA organizer.

2. Place the IDEA for Vocabulary Words transparency on the overhead. Write a word from your list in the first row under "Word." Have students say the word and copy it on their organizers.

3. In the *D* column, write the word's pronunciation as it appears in a dictionary, explaining symbols as needed. Have students copy this. Read the dictionary definition aloud and with the students, decide what part of speech the word is. Write this under the pronunciation and have students copy it. Elicit students' ideas, then rewrite the definition on the transparency in your own words and theirs. Have students copy this definition. Here's what the word *abdicate* might look like on the organizer under *D*.

    ab' di kāt

    verb

    give up power

IDEA for Vocabulary Words

Unit _Government–Monarchy_   Date _October 13_

	I **Illustrate** (picture or symbol)	D **Describe** (pronunciation, part of speech, and description)	E **Elaborate**	A **Associate** (personally meaningful sentence)
Word: abdicate	king abdicates his throne	ab' di kat verb give up power	Synonyms renounce relinquish	I had to abdicate my iPod because of my bad report card.
Word: dynasty		di' na stee noun powerful group that rules in succession	Synonyms royalty "a house"	I don't think I'd want to be a part of a dynasty since I like to do my own thing. I wouldn't want to inherit my job.
Word: monarchy		mon' ar kee noun form of government in which one person is in control	Synonyms ruler noble Example- King George	I'm glad we don't have a monarchy. I like our system of checks and balances.

4. Move to the *E* column to elaborate on the word. There are many ways to do this. Students may list synonyms, antonyms, examples, non-examples, or characteristics. Have each student turn to a neighbor and choose one way to elaborate on the word. Have students write their elaborations in the *E* column. For *abdicate*, for example, a student might write this:

   Synonyms

   renounce

   relinquish

5. Ask students to make personal associations with this word, connecting it to something they know, have read, or have seen on TV, in a movie, or on the Internet (see Tip). This is where students make the word personally meaningful and think independently; you should see smoke coming from their ears! Have them write a meaningful sentence in the *A* column.

6. Finally, have students go back and complete the *I* column independently by drawing a picture or symbol that will help them to understand and remember the word. This should be a simple drawing—just a quick sketch that represents their personal understanding. Have them use colored pencils or markers to enhance memory.

Tip

Here are some questions to ask students to spark an association.

- What words could be grouped with this word?
- To what concepts might this word be attached?
- What books, TV shows, Web sites, or games might be related to this word?
- What personal experience can you associate with this word?

Step-by-Step Instructions

1. Once students are comfortable with this process, have them work with a partner to complete the *E*, *A*, and *I* sections of their organizers for each need-to-know word. Always do the *D* section together so that no students misunderstand or get any misconceptions about the word. It takes 10 times more energy to unlearn wrong information than to learn new information!

2. Have students arrange their organizers in their three-ring binders by content area.

Checking for Understanding

- Collect students' binders and check for completeness and accuracy.
- Quiz students on words.
- Have students write a paragraph that contains some or all of the words. Remind them to use IDEA for Vocabulary Words as a resource when they write.

Ways to Differentiate Instruction

- For students who struggle with the pronunciation of unfamiliar words, teach the use of a pronunciation key to build confidence and word fluency.

- If pacing keeps students from completing all of the steps in the IDEA process, ask them to complete at least the *I*, *D*, and *A* columns.

IDEA for Vocabulary Words

Date _____

Word:	I **Illustrate** (picture or symbol)	D **Describe** (pronunciation, part of speech, and description)	E **Elaborate**	A **Associate** (personally meaningful sentence)
Word:				
Word:				
Word:				

IDEA Vocabulary Log

Name: _____

Class: _____

Date: _____

GROUPING SUGGESTION:
whole class, independent

TIME ALLOTMENT:
3–5 minutes

GRADE RANGE:
4–12

Off-the-Wall Word Wall

Academic words are those abstract but critical words that students must understand to complete assignments and assessments correctly. The most challenging academic words involve higher-level critical and creative thinking skills and include words such as *analysis*, *evaluation*, and *synthesis*. Students who know the content but don't grasp the academic language will have trouble showing you what they know, so it's vital that they understand these words. English language learners are especially likely to fall into this category. They may have learned particular content information in their primary language, but have no way to show you this if they fail to understand the demands of the academic language in English. This strategy focuses on academic language and helps students make it part of their lexicon. Once students understand the words, they keep a tally of how often each one is used in class discussions, reading, and writing. After a particular word has received a designated number of tally marks (we recommend 25), the word goes "off the wall" and into common usage, and another one takes its place.

Why It Works

Students can't own words until they can use them correctly in their speech and writing, and to do that, they need to see the words frequently, elaborate on their meanings, and be held accountable for using them. This strategy gets students to focus on academic language. The more often they notice and use the words, the sooner they will own them. Use the words later for review and reminders when individuals have trouble figuring out what they are being asked to do in an assignment or assessment. When you have words that aren't moving off the wall for quite some time, make them worth two tally marks each time they are used.

MATERIALS & PREPARATION

- Sentence strips or oak tag
- Markers in different colors

1. Cut the sentence strips or oak tag to make about twenty 6 x 10-inch cards. The cards should be large enough so that you can print the words big enough to be visible to all students.

2. Create a list of academic words that your students need to know, based on their readiness level. Use words from Bloom's Taxonomy or others, or search for academic language in teacher resources.

3. Write each of the words you've chosen in a different color marker on the word cards.

Academic Language for Your Off-the-Wall Word Wall

	Verbs	Nouns
Knowledge	list, define, describe	definition
Comprehension	explain, retell	illustration, interpretation
Application	dramatize, interview, paraphrase	prediction
Analysis	inspect, compare, survey	classification, inference
Synthesis	compose, role-play, generalize	design, revision, invention
Evaluation	judge, critique, rank	summary, recommendation

4. Set aside space on a bulletin board and label it "Off-the-Wall Word Wall."

5. Plan to teach about five words a week. That will get you through about twenty in a month.

Introducing the Activity

1. Explain to students the importance of understanding academic language. They need to understand academic words in order to show what they know. Tell them that you will teach four or five words each week and that once you have explicitly taught an academic word and given students examples of its use, you'll post it on the word wall.

2. Once a word is posted, students need to listen for it during lessons, videos, and class discussions. Tell them to watch for its appearance in assignments, assessments, and text. Explain that if a student hears the word during a lesson, or sees it in print, she should go to the word wall and make a tally mark on the word card when the lesson is over. You might nod in acknowledgment, but don't interrupt the flow of the class. Later, ask the student to share with the class how the word was used.

3. Explain that most people must use a word at least 25 times in context to make it part of their lexicon, so a card will stay on the wall until it has 25 tally marks. Then you'll move it off the wall and replace it with a new word card.

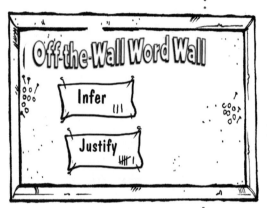

Tip

- Don't overload working memory. If students have trouble mastering these words, teach only two or three per week.
- In addition to giving students a description of the word, ask a volunteer to define it in his own words on another card and post it near the original card.
- Use IDEA (p. 73) to have students elaborate on a word's meaning, or choose another strategy from this book.
- If you want to use the word cards from year to year, laminate them or have students make their tally marks on a sticky note on each word card.

Checking for Understanding

- To make sure students understand a word, give them a short assignment in which the word is used in the directions. For example, you might ask them to "*appraise* the work ethic" of each of the three little pigs or "show in an *illustration* two safety rules to follow in a fire drill."

- Have students check with a classmate to make sure a word is being used correctly in writing or speaking before they make a tally mark on the word card.

- Check student understanding of academic language quickly with a formative assessment tool such as an exit ticket. Ask them to write a brief explanation of the term on a scrap of paper to give you on their way out the door. Have them initial the paper so that you can check in with them later if they seem to be having trouble with a word.

Ways to Differentiate Instruction

- To help visual learners remember the words, color code them by category or part of speech. Color enhances memory.

- English language learners may benefit from small-group instruction that focuses on identifying these words in text. Give them highlighting tape or sticky notes and let them skim textbooks or old assessments to identify academic language. Provide a list of the words you want them to focus on.

- At some point, you may want to categorize the academic words according to Bloom's Taxonomy. This helps students to understand the varying levels or degrees of difficulty they can expect to find in assessments. Knowing the demands of academic language can help them shape their responses to different kinds of questions.

T Chart for Analogy

Our students like using T charts—they offer a simple, visual way to begin comparing two dissimilar words, items, ideas, theories, or concepts. Organized students love the T chart's sequential nature, and those who need to be more organized find that it helps them to lay out their thinking visually. Once students have completed a T chart, they can rearrange the contents to better explain how two words are related. Our students' ideas and connections sometimes make us chuckle, but we're usually impressed with the connections they make. This is a great strategy to use during learning to help students process the concepts behind new vocabulary.

Why It Works

Analogies help familiarize students with concepts that are abstract and outside their previous realms of experience. To be effective, one part of the analogy must be very familiar to students so that they can compare the known properties with the properties of the target concept. Students first see this activity as a game and are very adept at finding the relationships between two "unlike" ideas, items, or terms. T charts are especially helpful for organizing the properties of the words being compared. In addition, graphic and symbolic representations of vocabulary words enhance students' understandings of the concepts behind the words.

MATERIALS & PREPARATION

- **Transparency**

1. Draw a simple T chart on a transparency.
2. Compile a list of vocabulary words that have strong concepts behind them.
3. Plan ahead and come up with several unrelated terms students could use for comparison with the vocabulary words. This list is just for your reference.
4. Decide how you'll distribute the words for the T charts: random draw, student choice, or teacher choice.

Introducing the Activity

1. Place the transparency on the overhead. Introduce a practice word or phrase for modeling the strategy. Let's use **invasive species**, from a unit on ecosystems, here.

2. Write the target phrase at the top of the left-hand column on the T chart. Use the illustration as a guide as you discuss and complete the chart in the following steps.

3. Discuss the meanings of **invasive** and **species**. As part of a unit on ecosystems, students have learned that an invasive species is a plant or animal that is not native to a particular area but that has overpopulated that area, with adverse effects. Brainstorm with students things that invade, or come into another's space, and list these on the board. Answers might include relatives, sports fans, aliens from space, and burglars. Choose one as the analogy phrase—let's use **visiting team's fans** here—and write it at the top of the right-hand column on the T chart.

4. With students, begin to list the properties of the target phrase in the left column and the properties of the analogy phrase in the right column.

T Chart for Analogy

TOPIC 1: Invasive Species

- *Not native to the area*
- *Might start small but can spread*
- *Not planted in the area on purpose*

TOPIC 2: Visiting Team's Fans

- *Not part of the local community*
- *Team comes in small numbers, but fans increase those numbers*

An invasive species is a species of plant that is brought into a biome but is not part of that biome naturally. The fans for a visiting team come to a different community to watch the team play but do not live in that community on a regular basis.

An invasive species may start as a small plant in the nonnative biome, but it takes root and begins to spread throughout the area. The fans of a visiting team begin to arrive in small numbers, but by the start of the game, the stadium is filled with visitors.

An invasive species isn't always planted on purpose in a biome, and generally the natives would like to see it disappear because it changes the biome. The visiting fans are invited for a period of time but are then expected to leave.

5. Have students discuss the two phrases and how they are related. Record their comments at the bottom of the transparency. Explain that they will have the opportunity to create and share their own T charts.

Step-by-Step Instructions

1. Give each student or pair of students one of the vocabulary words on your list. Have each student or pair of students draw a T chart similar to the one you drew on the transparency.

2. Have students write their target words at the top of the left column on the T chart and start brainstorming unrelated terms they could use for comparison. Offer feedback, using your list of comparison words. Possibilities might include *tornado* compared to *Twister ride at Six Flags*, or *Earth's rotation* compared to *ice-cream maker*. Have students write their analogy words at the top of the right column.

3. Tell students to begin listing the properties of the target word in the left column and the properties of the analogy word in the right column. Tell them that as they're doing this, they can also write supporting statements for why they placed the properties in either the left or the right column.

4. Have students write supporting paragraphs at the bottom of their T charts comparing the two words based on the properties listed. Remind them to include a topic sentence, supporting details, and a concluding sentence.

5. Allow time for students to share their T charts in groups or with the whole class.

Checking for Understanding

- For evaluation, have students answer the following questions about their T charts:
  * In how many ways were you able to compare or contrast these words?
  * Did the comparisons make sense with respect to both the target word and the analogy word? Explain.
  * How did the analogy extend your understanding of the vocabulary word?

- Evaluate the paragraphs students wrote on their T charts. Check for a topic sentence, supporting details that explain the comparisons, and a concluding sentence.

Ways to Differentiate Instruction

- For at-risk learners, scaffold instruction by selecting vocabulary that represents their levels of readiness and preteach the lesson in a small group. Additionally, consider using the T Chart Variation (see illustration). The teacher fills in the two words or concepts to be compared as well as the categories to be used for comparison on the stem of the T. This gives struggling learners a format to follow.

- To help kinesthetic learners process information, have them write the properties on sticky notes and manipulate them on the T chart while they talk about the comparisons.

T Chart Variation

Proteins		Dairy
2–3/day	Servings/Day	2–3/day
protein, iron, zinc, vitamin B	Nutrients	calcium, phosphorus, vitamin A, vitamin D
muscle of animals; beans, nuts	Source	milk of mammals
beef, chicken, pork, fish, eggs, dried beans, nuts, tofu	Examples	yogurt, cheese, milk
high in fat and cholesterol	Other Comments	high in fat; low-fat and nonfat versions available

Verb Energizers

Energize students for powerful learning opportunities by inviting them to participate in this activity throughout the day. It's as simple as creating a poster of unusual action verbs every month and then letting students *lollop* over to another group of students, *sashay* to the door, or *saunter* to their next class. The goal is to get students out of their chairs. Learning colorful verbs and adverbs is a bonus. Use this strategy whenever students' focus and attention dwindle and they need a brain break.

Why It Works

The research is definitive: physical activity oxygenates the brain and boosts cognition. Movement enhances energy, focus, and thinking, while novelty catches our attention. Especially in the upper grades, students spend too much time in chairs that allow for little movement. After an opportunity to exercise briefly—and energize their bodies and brains—they'll be ready for the learning opportunities ahead.

MATERIALS & PREPARATION

- Chart paper
- Bold markers in various colors
- Music (optional)

1. Choose 10 verbs from a particular content area, literature, the list on page 90, or the dictionary and use the markers to write them on chart paper in print that's large enough for all students to see.

2. Next to each word, write a brief definition.

3. Post this chart so that it's visible to all students.

4. Later, when students have learned the meanings of the verbs, add 10 adverbs to make the verbs more dynamic. Depending on your class, you might do this at the same time as you introduce the verbs.

Introducing the Activity

1. Read the first verb and its definition. Ask students to predict what it might look like. Ask for volunteers to stand up and demonstrate. If no one volunteers, demonstrate the verb yourself. For example, the word *lollop* means "to move with a bobbing motion". You might move slowly up and down by bending your knees rather than moving your feet. This is sure to get a few laughs, and laughter enhances learning!

2. If you're using adverbs at this point, add one to make your lolloping even more interesting. Maybe you'll *lollop lightly*.

3. Add a prepositional phrase with a location. You might *lollop lightly across the classroom*, for example. Adding background music may encourage student participation.

4. Teach and practice all the verbs on Monday and use them whenever a brain break is needed.

Step-by-Step Instructions

1. After you've taught a chunk of information, ask students to stand up. Call on one to choose a verb, another student to choose an adverb, and a third a location. Have the class follow the directions based on these choices.

2. Have students continue this energizer from 30 seconds to 2 minutes. For anyone who has been sitting too long or is out of shape, stretching new muscles and doing new movements can be difficult even for 30 seconds. You can invite other students to choose different words after a minute or so.

Ways to Differentiate Instruction

- Invite verbal-linguistic learners to focus on the action verbs they find in their reading for the day, then have these students add the verbs to the chart.

- Have visual learners, or those who need graphic reminders to process word meanings, create simple line drawings depicting the movement suggested by a verb. They might want to add these to their IDEA Vocabulary Logs (p. 73).

- For students who need more time to understand the verbs and their meanings, delay adding adverbs. Let them perform the actions alone until they're ready for more.

Verb Energizers

Try these with your students.

Verbs	**Adverbs**
bewail	aggressively
coax	boldly
creep	expeditiously
gaze	hopelessly
guffaw	lazily
hoist	lightly
lollop	patiently
saunter	rapidly
trudge	shakily
whirl	silently

Vocabulary Bookmark

When students are reading any text and come to an unfamiliar word, they can use the Vocabulary Bookmark organizer to document new learning. Since each student chooses different words to study based on her background knowledge, this strategy offers differentiation. Collecting vocabulary bookmarks daily as they read helps students build vocabulary. They can use them later on to study for summative assessments and to help move words into long-term memory.

Why It Works

Giving students choices motivates them! Letting each student choose which word to elaborate on allows the student to explore a word she doesn't know. Predicting word meanings through context enhances critical thinking and keeps students hooked: they want to see if their predictions were on target. When students use a new word in a personally meaningful sentence and create a graphic for it, they're making strong neural connections.

MATERIALS & PREPARATION

- Vocabulary Bookmark organizer (p. 95)
- 2 transparencies

1. Make several copies of the Vocabulary Bookmark on page 95 for each student and a transparency for modeling.
2. Find a page from a grade-level text with at least one word that will be unfamiliar to most of your students. Make a transparency of the page.

Introducing the Activity

1. Give each student a copy of the organizer.
2. Place the transparency of the text on the overhead and read it aloud, stopping at the unfamiliar word. Say the word and have students repeat it with you. Ask, "Have you ever heard of this word? What do you think it means?" Ask students to write the word in box 1 of the organizer as you model this on the Vocabulary Bookmark transparency. (You'll be switching back and forth between the text transparency and the Vocabulary Bookmark transparency.)
3. In box 2 of the bookmark transparency, model writing the book's title and the page and sentence where the word is found (see illustration). Give students time to complete box 2 of the organizer.
4. Say, "Since I'm not sure what **glum** means, I'm going to look at the other words in the sentence for a clue. It says that he was acting 'different' and that he was giving 'wiseacre answers,' so maybe **glum** means he's **sarcastic** or **negative**. I'm going to write those words in box 3 as related words." Ask students either to copy your words or to write their own predictions for the meaning of **glum** on their organizers.
5. Ask a volunteer to look up **glum** in a dictionary and read the definition aloud. Record the dictionary definition in box 4 of the transparency while students write it on their organizers. Ask, "How close was our prediction? What strategies did we use to predict the definition?"

Vocabulary Bookmark

Name _____Elise_____

1. Word:

glum

2. Book title, page number, sentence:

Maniac Magee, p. 65
"He was acting so different, all glum, and wiseacre answers."

3. Predicted definition or related words:

sarcastic
negative

4. Actual dictionary definition:

dreary, gloomy

5. Meaningful sentence using word:

I felt so glum on the cold, rainy day when I didn't have anyone to hang out with.

6. Picture or symbol:

6. Explain to students that later they'll work with a partner or independently and continue reading to complete boxes 5 and 6. In box 5, they'll write a sentence that relates to their lives and shows they understand the new word. In box 6, they'll draw a picture or symbol to help them remember the word. For now, just fill in boxes 5 and 6 (see illustration) and show them the completed transparency.

7. Discuss the completed bookmark and any questions students might have.

Step-by-Step Instructions

1. Give each student several copies of the organizer. Explain that they should complete an organizer for each new word they encounter.

2. Have students choose a book to read with a partner or independently. Tell them that when they come to an unfamiliar word, they should write it in box 1 of the organizer. If they're working with a partner, they should select the word together, but each student will complete her own organizer.

3. Have students complete boxes 2 through 4. Partners may write different predictions for the meaning of the word (box 3), but the dictionary definition (box 4) should be the same. Make sure students choose the correct dictionary definition based on how the word is used in the sentence. If the definition is unclear to a student, restate it for him.

4. Have students continue reading until they finish a chapter or come to a new section (for nonfiction text). Then have them complete boxes 5 and 6. Ask them to share their new words with the class if time permits.

5. Tell students to save their bookmarks in their IDEA Vocabulary Logs (p. 73).

Checking for Understanding

- Use the words for assessment after students have read a chapter or section. Based on grade level and readiness, decide how many words students should collect per chapter.
- Have students fold box 1 of their bookmarks under so that only boxes 2 through 6 are visible. Have them exchange bookmarks with a partner and each try to guess the other's word by reading the definitions and sentence or by looking at the picture or symbol. Then have them flip the bookmarks over to show only box 1. Tell them to give the definition, use the word in a meaningful sentence, or make a quick sketch representing the word.
- Check box 5 to make sure students have used their words correctly.

Ways to Differentiate Instruction

- If students are reading in a similar content area, have them share their words and learn words from others through discussions, games, and cooperative learning activities.
- Have students form small groups, then have each student choose a word and teach it to the others in the group.

- Add elaboration strategies, such as listing synonyms, antonyms, examples, or characteristics of the new words, so that students gain a deeper understanding of the words. Have students write these lists on the backs of their bookmarks.

Vocabulary Bookmark

Name _____

1. Word:

2. Book title, page number, sentence:

3. Predicted definition or related words:

4. Actual dictionary definition:

5. Meaningful sentence using word:

6. Picture or symbol:

Vocabulary Bookmark

Name _____

1. Word:

2. Book title, page number, sentence:

3. Predicted definition or related words:

4. Actual dictionary definition:

5. Meaningful sentence using word:

6. Picture or symbol:

GROUPING SUGGESTION:
whole class

TIME ALLOTMENT:
30 minutes

GRADE RANGE:
4–12

Webbing the Content

It's all about connections. You might find yourself using this strategy more than any other in this book because of its multiple benefits for you and your students. Before you begin a unit, create a web of all the words and concepts you plan to teach and expect your students to master based on your state or district standards. This web will show students how all the concepts and terms are connected. Knowing what your summative assessment will look like will guide your choices. Your students will continue to refine their webs during the unit of study as they gain understanding and mastery.

Why It Works

Neural networks build on other neural networks, and similar information is stored together in the brain. Webs help the brain to see the big picture, so connections are better understood. This strategy helps students to see how terms and concepts are related. Ask them to write or discuss how and why words are related after they've worked with their webs for several weeks, and you'll be amazed at their knowledge. When your students can do this, you'll know they own the words.

MATERIALS & PREPARATION

- Large poster board
- Colored vis-à-vis markers
- Colored pencils

The illustration shows a concept web with "GEOMETRY" at the center, connected to categories: Rotate/Turn/Flip, Congruent, Similar, Space Figures (Cube, Prism, Pyramid, Cylinder, Cone, Sphere; Face, Edge, Vertex), Lines (Point, Ray, Line, Line segment, Plane, Intersecting, Parallel), Angles (Vertex, Acute, Obtuse, Right, Straight, Perpendicular), and Polygons (Triangle–3, Quadrilateral–4, Pentagon–5, Hexagon–6, Heptagon–7, Octagon–8, Decagon–10; Equilateral, Isosceles, Scalene; Trapezoid, Rectangle, Square, Parallelogram, Rhombus).

1. A web has one central concept; our example uses "geometry" (see illustration). The next-largest concepts extend out from this. These secondary categories have many specific words listed below them in the web.

2. Brainstorm all the words and concepts students need to know by the end of a unit based on state or district standards. Group these according to similarity: Which words are related and would be taught in a particular lesson? Which words share a category? Use teacher resource books or the curriculum guide to choose concepts and related vocabulary words.

3. Make your web on large poster board. Use different colors to code related words or concepts. Laminate it so that students can add to it with vis-à-vis markers as the unit progresses.

4. Draw a copy of your web on a sheet of 8 ½ x 11-inch paper and make copies for students.

Introducing the Activity

1. Show students the web poster you've created. Describe the interesting lessons and projects they'll be doing throughout this unit as you point out each part of the web.

2. Review each section of your web, explaining how one chunk of information relates to another. Ask students, "What do you already know about the words on this part of the web?" This accomplishes two goals: it primes your students' brains so they can start to access prior knowledge about the content, and it serves as a general preassessment of what they already know (or what misinformation they might have).

3. Tell students that they will be adding more words to the web poster throughout the unit to support their learning. Post the web with vis-à-vis markers nearby so that students can add to it.

Step-by-Step Instructions

1. Before each lesson in the unit, say, "Explain to me where we were in our work yesterday." Allow time to discuss and review previous material. Then tell students what they will be learning today and ask them how the new topic might relate to what they have already learned. What connections can they make to words and concepts taught previously?

2. Give each student a copy of the web. Tell students that they will be adding to their webs during the unit and that they can use colored pencils to code chunks of related information at the end of each lesson. (Allow a few minutes for this immediately after each lesson while the information is still fresh.)

3. At the conclusion of the unit, have students place their webs in their IDEA Vocabulary Logs (p. 73).

Tip

Continually refer to the web whenever you teach a new word in a unit so that students are always seeing the connections among the words and how they relate to each other.

Checking for Understanding

- At the end of the unit, assess learning with a cloze technique. Cover some of the words on the web and have students write the missing words on sticky notes and place them in the best locations. Have students explain and defend their placements. To make this an individual assessment, use a copy of the web you gave students, white out some of the words, recopy the web, and then have them write in the missing words.

- Create essay questions that require students to visualize the web in order to answer the questions. Remind them to think visually about their individual webs to access information.

Ways to Differentiate Instruction

- To encourage students to think critically, show them your web but give them only the main topic and ask them to create their own webs. Then have them compare and contrast their webs with yours. Doing this with a partner or in small groups will jump-start students who have prior knowledge but may have trouble accessing it.

- For students who need organizational help, create unit books in which all notes and handouts are placed for easy review. Glue a copy of the 8 ½ x 11-inch version of the web on the front inside cover page so that students can refer to it.

- Have visual learners add illustrations, sketches, or diagrams to their webs to help them recall the information and deepen their understanding of words.

Part Three

Vocabulary Strategies to Use After Learning

GROUPING SUGGESTION:
independent or partners

TIME ALLOTMENT:
15–30 minutes

GRADE RANGE:
4–12

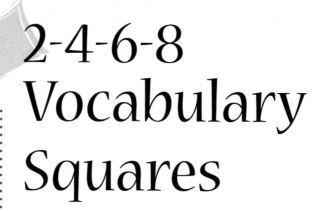

2-4-6-8 Vocabulary Squares

2-4-6-8 Vocabulary Squares was designed to help students understand words based on their individual background knowledge. Students can create their own graphic organizers with 2, 4, 6, or 8 squares for processing (making sense and meaning of) a vocabulary word. When you let them choose how they want to process a word's meaning or elaborate on their vocabulary words, you empower students, and that's motivating!

Why It Works

The more ways a student elaborates on a word, the more in-depth she understands its meaning. Students remember words better when learning starts where their background knowledge begins—a scaffolding approach. They need something to hang new learning on! Giving students choices in how they want to take ownership of new words motivates them to participate in the activities, too. This strategy encourages students to choose the best ways for them to elaborate on words they need to learn, so their processing time is maximized. When students are allowed to choose, they usually base their choices on their interests or comfort level; both increase motivation. An added bonus is that the process of choosing is in itself a metacognitive activity.

MATERIALS & PREPARATION

- 2-4-6-8 Vocabulary Squares Ideas reproducible (p. 106)
- 2-4-6-8 Vocabulary Squares organizer (p. 107)
- 8 ½ x 11-inch sheets of photocopier paper
- Colored pencils or markers (optional)

1. Make copies of 2-4-6-8 Vocabulary Squares Ideas and a transparency of 2-4-6-8 Vocabulary Squares (p.107) for modeling.

2. Preassess your students' knowledge of a set of words from a unit or lesson. (For a preassessment idea, see Levels of Knowing, p. 29.) Based on the results, create a list of words that need more elaboration for students to understand them in-depth. Use a variety of words for different readiness and instructional levels and interests. Make copies of the list for students.

Introducing the Activity

1. Give each student a copy of the reproducible and a blank sheet of paper.

2. Tell students that there are many ways to elaborate on a word and its meaning. Read through the list of ideas on the reproducible and describe what each idea might look like. Give examples where appropriate and model creating several of the ideas on the board or overhead. Share an example of a completed activity (see illustration) so that students know how to create this graphic organizer.

3. Share with students a word they'll need to understand from your prepared list. For example, they would need to fully understand **fault** for a unit on volcanoes and earthquakes.

4. Demonstrate how to hold the paper landscape style, fold it to make three columns, and then fold it in half to create 6 equal boxes. Have students do this, then ask them to use rulers to draw a straight line over each fold line. (We've chosen 6 boxes for this example, but you can also make 2, 4, or 8 boxes, depending on grade level and time available.)

2-4-6-8 Vocabulary Squares

Name _Michael_   Word _properties_

Definitions	Word in context	Meaningful Sentence
a characteristic of a substance a quality peculiar to something	Describe three properties of chemical change.	My bike has these properties: blue paint, two round wheels, two hand brakes, a metal frame.
Synonyms attributes qualities traits	Illustrate Word	Examples sight sound color number appearance texture fragrance taste shape size

5. Have students write the word *fault* at the top of their papers.

6. Go back to the list of ideas and say, "Let's choose six ways from this list to elaborate on this word. A different choice will go inside each box." Ask students to read through the list silently and place stars next to six ways they would like to elaborate on the word *fault*.

7. Call on students to share which ideas they starred. Write six or seven of their choices on the board. For example:
    *   Illustrate the word.
    *   List characteristics of the word.
    *   Create a "what if" question with the word.
    *   Create a pun using the word.
    *   Create a simile.
    *   Use the word in an analogy.

8. Direct students to record a different idea at the top of each box on their papers. Explain that they should shorten the idea—for example, "Definitions" for "Define it in your own words"—because the rest of the space in each box is for elaborating on the word in that way.

9. Have students choose partners and use texts, reference books, dictionaries, glossaries, and thesauruses to complete each square.

10. Allow time for sharing the completed organizers as a class. Students will get good ideas from seeing what their classmates have done.

Step-by-Step Instructions

1. Give each student a sheet of paper and a copy of the vocabulary list. Have students choose a vocabulary word from the list, or you may assign words based on the students' individual preassessment results (a word that would be "just right" for them).

2. Ask students to create a graphic organizer based on how they want to process the word. The following suggestions may help with this process:
    *   2 boxes for students who have shown little or no background knowledge of the word or would be overwhelmed by too many tasks

- 4 or 6 boxes for students who have some background knowledge of the word
- 8 boxes for students who are comfortable with the word and are ready for deeper understanding

3. Tell students to use 2-4-6-8 Vocabulary Squares Ideas to choose how they will process their words. They may choose ideas from each list or only from the list that you feel best meets their readiness level. Allow for student choice, but also guide students so that those who are ready for challenges seek them, while those who need more basic understanding will get it.

4. Have students write their choices in shortened form at the top of each square, making sure to save room for their work. Then have them complete each box. Encourage them to use color to enhance memory.

5. Ask students to share their completed organizers in small groups.

Checking for Understanding

Use the following criteria to evaluate students' work:

- The word's meaning is accurately represented.
- Each square is completed with a different idea.
- The student can discuss the word and use it correctly.
- The final product demonstrates thoughtful consideration.
- The student used different resources (thesaurus for synonyms, dictionary for multiple meanings).
- The student can teach the word to others.

Ways to Differentiate Instruction

The three lists of ideas on page 106 function as differentiated activities. List A ideas are the easiest, while List C contains the most complex ways to elaborate on words. Use the three lists to scaffold learning for at-risk learners. In addition, you can preselect the words you want struggling students to explore, or give them fewer words when you start this strategy.

2-4-6-8 Vocabulary Squares Ideas

List A: Ideas for Understanding the Basics of a Word

- Define it in your own words.
- Illustrate the word.
- Write a meaningful sentence.
- List characteristics of the word.
- Create a rhyme, pun, or cartoon.
- List synonyms.
- List antonyms.
- List other meanings for the word.
- List words with the same spelling pattern.

List B: Ideas for Analyzing and Applying a Word

- How and when would you use the word?
- List three examples of the word.
- Web the word to four related words or concepts.
- List two ways you might use the word in the future.
- Use the word in a question or an exclamatory sentence.
- Divide the word into syllables; mark the stressed syllable.
- Add a prefix or suffix. Explain how the word's meaning changes.
- Create a simile or metaphor.
- Use the word in an analogy.
- Summarize what you know about the word in a sentence.

List C: Ideas for Evaluating and Synthesizing the Word

- What are your opinions and feelings about the word?
- Connect the word to your life.
- How does the word relate to current world events?
- Create a "what if" question with the word.
- List the pros and cons of the word.
- Rate the word 1, 2, or 3 based on how important you think it is for this unit. Explain.
- Create an acronym to explain what it means.
- Research the etymology (history) of the word.

2-4-6-8 Vocabulary Squares

Name _____

Word _____

10-24-7 Review

Based on research about how often the brain needs to review information before it gets into long-term memory, we created 10-24-7 Review—a brain-compatible way to review words. Students review words approximately 10 minutes after a lesson, 24 hours later (the next day), and again 7 days later. This system not only helps students to master vocabulary but also keeps your review of words consistent. You'll find that students tend to use the words more often in their speech and writing, too!

Why It Works

Research suggests that neural connections become stronger the more neurons fire and are wired together in consistent patterns. To create strong connections between new neurons, the brain benefits from reviewing new content right after it is learned, 24 hours later, and 7 days later. This doesn't mean that reviewing stops at this point. The saying "use it or lose it" is certainly true for vocabulary words.

MATERIALS & PREPARATION

- Shoe box
- Oak tag
- Several packs of 3 x 5-inch index cards
- Colored markers
- Pocket chart (approximately 40 x 58 inches; optional)

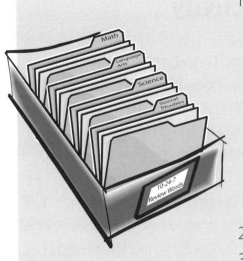

1. To make dividers for the shoe box, cut the oak tag into cards that fit neatly in the box. The dividers should be taller than the index cards, so they stand above the cards, and have a tab on the top right (see illustration). Make one divider for each subject that you teach. For example, if you teach American history, geography, and Middle East history, you'll need three dividers. Write a subject on each divider, using a different-colored marker for each. Put the dividers in the box. If you teach at the elementary level, you'll need different-colored markers for social studies, science, language arts, and math.

2. Hang up the pocket chart (or create your own; see Tip).

3. Use colored tape (electrical tape works well) to divide the pocket chart into a table with six columns and one row for each subject you teach. In the first column, list the subjects that you teach. Label the other five columns Monday through Friday at the top.

Tip

You can easily make your own pocket chart. On a bulletin board, use strips of paper or colored electrical tape to create a table with six columns—one column on the far left for the subjects you teach and five columns labeled Monday through Friday—and a row for each subject (see below). Use thumbtacks to attach the labels and words to the bulletin board.

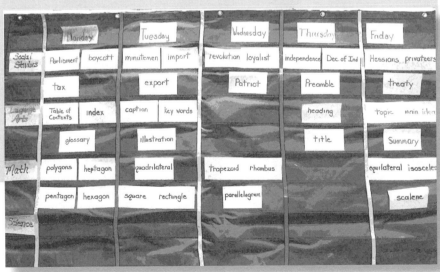

Introducing the Activity

1. Explain to students that to hold on to words they have studied, they need to review the words. Describe to them the three parts of the 10-24-7 Review strategy and explain how each part will help them to plant learning in their long-term memories. When you have led them through the first review and they understand how it works, the students themselves can lead the activity each day.

2. Ask for three or four student volunteers to manage the reviewing system for a month. (You can rotate this job so that all the students get a chance.)

10-Minute Review

1. About 10 minutes after teaching your math lesson on Monday, for example, ask students to tell you the vocabulary words that were taught. As they do, have your student managers write each word on a 3 x 5-inch index card in the color you've assigned to this subject. For example, all math-related words are written in blue marker.

2. Ask the class to generate accurate definitions of these words based on what they learned in the lesson.

3. Have the managers write an agreed-upon definition on the back of each word card, then place the cards in the pocket chart under Monday in the math row.

4. You might teach a social studies lesson next. Again, after the lesson, ask students to brainstorm the words that were taught. Have the managers write them on cards in a different-colored marker (for example, red for social studies). Have students generate definitions and when one is agreed upon a manager writes the definition on the back of each card. Then the cards are placed in the appropriate pocket—under Monday in the social studies row.

5. Repeat this process after every lesson every day. Remember, this is just for new words that are part of your curriculum or that you've identified as priority words.

24-Hour Review

1. On Tuesday, ask a student manager to stand up and take 5 minutes to review Monday's words. Establish a routine for doing the 24-hour review; revisiting words taught the previous day should occur at a specified time every day. Have the student manager say the word on the card and call on classmates who raise their hands to explain its meaning. Tell the manager that she can get creative and ask the class to elaborate on the word in any of the following ways:

   - Give an example of the word.
   - Give a non-example of the word.
   - Describe attributes of the word.
   - Use the word in a different way from the original text.
   - Give synonyms for the word.
   - Give antonyms for the word.
   - Tell what you know about the word in 30 seconds.
   - On the board, sketch a picture or symbol of the word.
   - Explain how the word relates to your life.
   - Relate the word to current events.

2. Make a list of these options and post it near your pocket chart for quick reference.

7-Day Review

1. After the Monday morning review, have the student managers take all of the cards out of the pockets and file them behind the appropriate dividers in the shoe box. Now the chart can be used for the current week's vocabulary words.

2. Every day at the end of class, take a few minutes to review the filed words in one subject area. On Monday, you might review five to seven math words. This review is similar to the 24-hour review. After the review, have the student managers place the word cards used that day at the back of the subject section in the box. That way, the cards will be rotated and all of the words will get reviewed about 7 days after they were introduced.

3. Do this again on Tuesday, but with cards from a different

subject area. Keep the rotation going, and eventually the words will be reviewed 1 month later, then 6 months later. The elaboration part of the review will help plant the information in long-term memory.

Checking for Understanding

- Give periodic quizzes that include the words. Assess for in-depth understanding of the words rather than rote definitions.
- Ask students to write a paragraph or essay that has a specific purpose (e.g., informational writing, persuasive writing) and includes some of the words used appropriately and effectively.
- Listening to how individual students respond to the reviews and making anecdotal notes will give you insight about their levels of understanding and help you to design instruction for reteaching or clarification for small groups of students.

Ways to Differentiate Instruction

- For students who struggle with oral responses, particularly English language learners, read the definitions to them, then ask them to give you the words.
- Ask verbal-linguistic learners to create similes, metaphors, or analogies using the new words.

- Have students who are ready for more challenging elaborations explore the etymology of the words.

GROUPING SUGGESTION:
partners

TIME ALLOTMENT:
20 minutes

GRADE RANGE:
4–12

Extreme Vocabulary

As students move into adolescence, they begin to see the world as black and white, with few shades of gray in between. This strategy asks students to focus on the extremes of concepts, then explore words that describe degrees in between. The kinesthetic and ongoing aspects of this activity also help students learn through an alternate pathway and build on their knowledge as they locate new words to fill in the continuum. Extreme Vocabulary is a great way for students to evaluate new vocabulary words after a lesson.

Why It Works

Students like extremes. Just think about the drama queens (and kings) in your class. They can exaggerate with drama and flair—the best, the worst, the happiest, or the saddest. Students usually express the superlative by adding *est* to an adjective, but that's because they lack more precise language. This strategy asks them to focus on more accurate and specific words. Students enjoy manipulating the word cards on the continuum, and knowing that the placement may change when a new word appears aids processing as they consider and discuss each word's placement.

MATERIALS & PREPARATION

- Transparency
- Yarn or tape for bulletin board lines
- Slips of paper

1. Turn a blank transparency landscape style and draw a horizontal line across the center.

2. Make a list of several pairs of vocabulary words that express extremes—for example, *black/white*, *happy/sad*, *new/old*, *cold/hot*. Most opposites work well.

3. Dedicate a bulletin board to Extreme Vocabulary for a period of time. Use yarn or tape to create a horizontal continuum for each pair of vocabulary words. Write the words on slips of paper and staple each pair to opposite ends of a continuum.

Introducing the Activity

1. Introduce a pair of words for practice—for example, *small* and *large*. Explain that to describe people, animals, objects, or even ideas, we sometimes use words that are at opposite ends of a continuum. To describe an apple, for example, one person might say that it's *small* and another that it's *large*. Write these words on the transparency at either end of the horizontal line.

2. Explain that one person also might describe the taste of the apple as *sweet* and another as *tart*. These words also are at opposite ends of a continuum. Draw another horizontal line on the transparency and write the words at opposite ends of it.

3. Tell students that there are many words they can use to describe size other than *small* and *large* or taste other than *sweet* and *tart*. Some words might describe smaller than small and others larger than large. There are also words that would describe all the sizes in between.

4. Ask students to find partners and together think of words that fit somewhere on the continuum between *small* and *large*.

5. After a few minutes, ask each pair to share their words. As they suggest a word, ask them where on the continuum they think it should be placed and have them explain why. This discussion of words and their nuanced meanings is important. Students learn

from one another, and they're actively processing meanings as they listen and talk.

6. As each pair suggests a word for the continuum and explains their reasoning, make additions to and placement changes along the continuum based on their suggestions. Continue until all pairs have had an opportunity to offer a word or until the line is filled with words.

Step-by-Step Instructions

1. Give each set of partners a pair of vocabulary words to explore.

2. Have students begin by brainstorming a list of descriptive terms that could be placed on the continuum between the two extremes. They may use a thesaurus, a dictionary, Web sites (see p. 140 for some great ones), and any other resources to find words. Have them write each word on a slip of paper and attach their slips to the line on the bulletin board. (See illustration.)

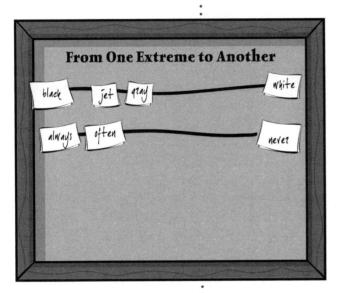

From One Extreme to Another

3. Over the next few days, have each pair of students share their word continuum with the class. Ask them to stand by their continuum and read their words.

4. When students use these words in their speech or written work, be sure to take note of it and congratulate them.

Checking for Understanding

As an evaluative activity, give each student a pair of words that would go at opposite ends of a continuum. Give each student a sheet of paper and ask students to draw a horizontal line in the middle of the paper and write one word at each end. Then have them write words along the continuum, using a dictionary or thesaurus for help. Have them write a paragraph at the bottom of the paper explaining why they placed the words where they did—that is, what subtle differences caused them to place one word before or after another.

Ways to Differentiate Instruction

- For visual and kinesthetic students, use paint-sample cards from a home decorating store and have students arrange the cards by color hue or intensity, the darkest sample at one end of the continuum and the lightest at the other. If you use cards without paint color names, ask your verbal-linguistic learners to assign names to the colors. They'll enjoy comparing their names to the actual ones used by the paint company. This may lead to a powerful discussion about marketing.

- To scaffold learning, give students slips of paper or sticky notes with a series of words that would fall between two extremes already written on them. They must decide where to place the words along the continuum, using a dictionary and discussions with a partner to find the subtle differences in the words' meanings. You'll find several lists you can use on page 117. Copy the words from a list onto sticky notes, or reproduce the page and cut the words into separate slips of paper to give to students.

Extreme Vocabulary

From One Extreme to Another

- black
- jet
- ebony
- sable
- charcoal
- gray
- eggshell
- ivory
- white

- thrilled
- blissful
- happy
- content
- unhappy
- sad
- melancholic
- depressed
- distraught
- heartbroken
- inconsolable

- minute
- microscopic
- tiny
- small
- average
- big
- large
- huge
- immense
- gargantuan

- always
- often
- frequently
- sometimes
- occasionally
- rarely
- seldom
- never

- freezing
- cold
- chilly
- cool
- mild

- tepid
- warm
- stifling
- hot
- boiling

List, Sort, Label & Write

Teachers are often surprised to find that they learn more about their students' understanding of vocabulary through List, Sort, Label & Write than they expected. Any student can give a rote definition, but this strategy drives students to a deeper level of understanding. Teachers also find that this strategy enhances their questioning techniques by encouraging thoughtful questions and then giving students time to think and talk. Students discuss what they are learning, listen to others' perspectives, and work collaboratively to decide on word placement. List, Sort, Label & Write is a great review but also helps build comprehension during learning.

Why It Works

Researchers who study how the brain learns new words note that concept-based vocabulary instruction has the most impact. When used during a unit of study, this strategy activates students' knowledge through word association and helps them to organize it in a systematic way. Students develop a deeper understanding of word meanings rather than rote memorization. This strategy also encourages students to take on different roles in a cooperative group and gives them opportunities to work together while making sense of new content.

MATERIALS & PREPARATION

- List, Sort, Label & Write Evaluation reproducible (p. 124)
- Transparency (optional)
- Word cards made out of transparency sheets or slips of paper
- Sticky notes

1. Make a copy of List, Sort, Label & Write Evaluation for each group and one for each student.

2. Choose a unit that students have completed and compile a list of vocabulary words. You may preselect the words to be used by each group and make a copy for the group (ready to be cut into strips). Or students can brainstorm words (using the textbook, if you want). As students call out words, write them on a chart or a transparency on the overhead. Later, when students are in their groups, have them divide up the words (or assign each group a list of words), then write them on slips of paper.

3. Be prepared to model how to group words under headings. You can model the strategy by using word cards made of transparency sheets on an overhead or slips of paper on the floor or a table so everyone can see, then sorting the words into groups.

Introducing the Activity

1. Present the topic (for example, biomes) to students. Ask them to brainstorm for a minute all the words they associate with the topic and record them on paper.

2. When a minute has passed, have students share their lists with a neighbor and then with the class. Record the words on the marker board or have a student do this. The collective list contains the target words each group will use for sorting.

3. Divide students into groups and have them choose roles so that everyone shares responsibility for the work ahead. Good roles for this activity include group manager, materials manager, and recorder. Explain that within each group, members will share the responsibility of getting the words copied on slips of paper for sorting. Show students how a sheet of paper can be folded in half multiple times to create many slips and torn with a ruler or against the side of a table. The group manager will make sure that this task is completed.

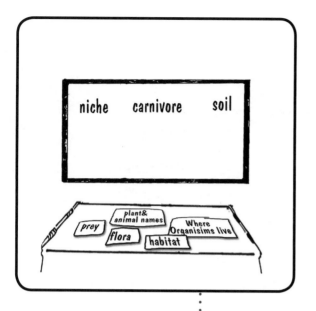

4. Tell the materials managers to arrange the word slips on the table so that all the group members can see them and can begin thinking about sorting possibilities.

5. Model how words might be grouped together. Laying out all the words for students to see, pick up one word—for example, *carnivore*, and say, "A carnivore is an animal that eats meat. Are there other words here that are similar in description or function that I could group with *carnivore*?" Call on a student who has found a word that could go with *carnivore*. Ask him to say his word and explain why it goes with *carnivore*. Ask, "What could the label for this group be?" When students decide on a possible label, such as "Plant and Animal Names," write it on a sticky note and place it above the group of words. Explain that this label may change as more words are sorted.

6. Teach students the language needed to negotiate moving a word from one category to another.

   • "I think the word could fit here because . . ."
   • "I understand what you are saying, but also . . ."
   • "I looked at the word in another way and . . ."

7. Engage them in a discussion on coming to a consensus and ask, "When you have only a few minutes to make a decision, what kind of reasoning might help you decide on a word's placement?"

8. Continue picking up words that might fit in the same category. When a student suggests a different category, start a new group by labeling a sticky note with another heading. Ask questions such as these:

   • Are there other words that are related to that idea?
   • What other categories would work with these words?
   • Are these two categories connected in any way?

Step-by-Step Instructions

1. Arrange students in mixed-ability groups to facilitate diverse conversations. Give each group and each student a copy of List, Sort, Label & Write Evaluation. Make sure each group has a list of target words. Have them cut apart the list or write the words on slips of paper.

2. Have each group sort the target words into categories, then label each category with a sticky note.

3. Have students discuss why particular words fit under specific headings, then negotiate the final placement of words when there are disagreements. Eventually, students will be able to organize the words under appropriate headings.

4. Move from group to group, asking about word placement and how the words relate. This is a great time to observe students interacting, to probe for deeper responses by giving them processing time, and to listen carefully while making anecdotal notes. Taking notes will remind you of the mini-lessons that need to be taught regarding concepts, sorting strategies, and skills such as diplomacy.

5. Ask a question such as "Why does this word fit in this category?" Wait for a complete explanation that includes a description of the word and how it relates to the category. Other questions to spur discussion include the following:
    *   Why does this category work within this larger concept?
    *   How does this word (pull a word card from a category) relate to this word (pull a word from a different category)?
    *   What additional words could you add to this sorting?
    *   In what other categories could this word (pull a card from a category) be placed?

6. Ultimately, every group member is responsible for knowing why the words are placed in their respective categories. The process (discussing and manipulating words; compromising and negotiating agreements) is more important than the product. Remind students that there are different answers for this activity.

7. Ask each recorder to complete the evaluation sheet, with help from all group members. Then have each student complete the individual evaluation section.

Checking for Understanding

- Assess the groups' work using the following criteria:
  * Did students cooperate?
  * Did they stay on task?
  * Did they accomplish the assigned task?
  * Did each member play a role and make a contribution?
  * Could students explain how they processed the work?

- As a culminating activity, have each student choose one category from his group's final categories and write an explanation of how the words in that category relate to one another and to the main topic. Criteria for assessing this written piece might include the following:
  * States a clear purpose for a word's placement in a specific category
  * Gives a clear definition or description of the vocabulary word and the category
  * Adequately describes the relationships between words in the category and between words and the main topic

Ways to Differentiate Instruction

- Give groups premade category labels to use for guiding word placement. The labels can be simple if you've chosen to group students homogeneously, or they can be designed with higher-thinking skills in mind.

- If you have a group that appears to be overwhelmed by the number of words, scoop up half of their word slips. When they're ready, give them the rest.

Biomes
Collective List

herbivore	prey	flora
ecosystem	food chain	fauna
niche	carnivore	overfishing
habitat	water	omnivore
consumer	soil	producer
predator	invasive species	food web

Plant and Animal Names
- omnivore
- carnivore
- predator
- prey
- consumer
- herbivore
- producer

Where Organisms Live
- habitat
- niche
- soil
- water

Problems
- overfishing
- invasive species

Relationships
- food chain
- food web

List, Sort, Label & Write Evaluation

Group members _____

Date _____ Assignment _____

GROUP EVALUATION

CRITERIA		1	2	3	4
Contributions	1. Members contribute equally to the task at hand.				
Cooperation	2. Members work well together, assisting one another as needed.				
On-Task Behavior	3. Team is on task and does not need teacher reminders.				
Communication	4. Members listen and speak to one another in friendly and encouraging tones.				

1. Not true of our group.
2. Working on this, but need more time to perfect the skill.
3. Putting this into practice.
4. True of us—awesome!

INDIVIDUAL EVALUATION

CRITERIA		1	2	3	4
Contributions	1. I contributed good ideas and information.				
Cooperation	2. I cooperated with and assisted others when they needed help.				
On-Task Behavior	3. I stayed focused and used time wisely.				
Communication	4. I listened to other group members and used friendly, encouraging language.				
Responsibility	5. I successfully performed my assigned role in the group.				

1. Not true of me.
2. Working on this, but need more time to perfect the skill.
3. Putting this into practice.
4. True of me—awesome!

Nonsense Books

Students love making these mini-books, which are a great way to help them enjoy, predict, and review word meanings. Students write sentences that make sense and use the vocabulary words from the content area or unit. Next, they replace the vocabulary word in each sentence with a nonsense word such as **dingledot**. Then they exchange their mini-books with a partner. Partners must guess which vocabulary word each nonsense word has replaced based on the context and the meaning in the sentence. It's a great way to review, and everyone enjoys a good laugh. Use this strategy at the end of a unit to help important words find their way into long-term memory.

Why It Works

Laughter creates and opens pathways to learning, while reviewing concepts and creating contextual, meaningful sentences enhance understanding and memory. This strategy is a good way to get those need-to-know words into long-term memory, and students love it!

MATERIALS & PREPARATION

- 5 x 9-inch or other size paper (Use up your scrap paper.)
- Transparency

1. Give each student enough sheets of paper to have one for each vocabulary word plus two more for cover pages.
2. Ask students to assemble their mini-books by placing the sheets together and stapling them at the top.

3. Make a list of vocabulary words for review, then give each student a copy of the list.

Introducing the Activity

1. Model for students how to create a sentence that uses a vocabulary word from the list. You might write the following sentence on the transparency:

   Britain put taxes on legal papers and imports, or goods brought into the country from another country.

   Point out to students that even if a reader did not know the meaning of the word ***imports***, he could figure it out by paying close attention to the context clue that follows the word, ***goods brought into the country.***

2. Explain that students will substitute a made-up word for the vocabulary word that's defined by the context clue—in this case, ***imports.*** Ask for volunteers to suggest a nonsense word or supply your own. Let's say you decide that ***sholala*** will replace ***imports***. Erase ***imports*** on the transparency and write the nonsense word in its place. Read the new sentence aloud or ask a volunteer to read it. (This is always good for a laugh.) Students should see that even though they've never heard of ***sholala***, they can figure out its meaning because of the context clue.

3. Write another example of a sentence with a context clue, but this time don't write the vocabulary word at all; use a made-up word instead. Have students read your sentence and try to figure out which vocabulary word your nonsense word stands for. For example, you might write:

   During the American War of Independence, nearly 20,000 German kaboodly troops, hired and paid to fight by the British, fought against the colonists on American soil.

Tip

This strategy works best if you've already taught your students the lesson Collecting Context Clues (p. 62). If not, just review these clues and give plenty of examples first. See page 67 for a list of kinds of context clues students can use with their sentences.

4. Draw a line on the transparency below the sentence and ask a volunteer to write the correct vocabulary word on the line. Students should be able to identify *mercenary* as the correct word based on the context clue *hired and paid to fight*.

Step-by-Step Instructions

1. Have each student choose a vocabulary word from the list for the first page of her book. Ask students to write a sentence using a nonsense word in place of the real word. The sentence must include a context clue that explains the meaning of the word. Tell them to draw a line below the sentence; this is where a partner will write the real word. If necessary, brainstorm with students a few silly but appropriate nonsense words to get them started.

2. Have students choose a word for each of the remaining pages of their mini-books and follow the same process. You may have them use every word on the list or only some of them. Remind them to vary the types of context clues on every page and to work neatly because another student will be reading their sentences to figure out the correct words. The other student and the teacher will be assessing their books as well.

3. When students have written a sentence on each page, have them create an answer key on a sheet of lined paper that is the same size as the pages of their mini-books. The key will be used to assess the accuracy of their sentences and the appropriateness of their context clues. Tell them to place the answer keys in the back of their books.

4. When they are finished, have students pair up and exchange books. Tell them to read through each other's books, try to figure out which vocabulary word each nonsense word represents, and then write their answers on the blank lines on each page.

Checking for Understanding

- Evaluate each book using the following checklist:
  - ❋ Correct use of each vocabulary word
  - ❋ Effective context clues
  - ❋ Variety of context clues
  - ❋ Answer line on each page
  - ❋ Answer key
  - ❋ Creative and varied sentence length and structure

- Have the author and the student reader evaluate the book as well using the same criteria.

Ways to Differentiate Instruction

- Have verbal-linguistic learners create a story with the context clues and nonsense words instead of separate sentences.

- For students who struggle to think of nonsense words, have a list ready so that they can concentrate on the most important part of the task—writing contextual sentences. Here are a few suggestions: *travity*, *simitate*, *pomino*, *tenemy*, *fruise*, *bagnoose*, *pilgritts*, and *sproon.*

- For students struggling with the content, provide resource materials where they can find sentences using the words from the list. Point out sentences that already have context clues for the target words. Have them copy the sentences and substitute nonsense words for the target words. They'll learn the content and identify context clues while also successfully completing the task.

- Give visually creative students the option of drawing a diagram of the content topic, using nonsense words instead of vocabulary words as labels. For example, a student might draw the water cycle and substitute nonsense words for *condensation* and *evaporation.*

Sum-Acrostic

Students love acrostic poems because they provide a structure that's easy to follow and the content is easy to write—it comes straight from their own lives. By fourth grade, most students are familiar with writing acrostics based on the letters in their names, so they have a sense of how to do this. This strategy focuses on a specific concept in an area of study and gives students a user-friendly format for presenting or showcasing new information that they have mastered.

Why It Works

Because acrostics limit how many words students can use, they must dig deeper into their understanding of the concepts behind a word. They also must summarize what they've learned about the concept, and that requires students to analyze the information in their notes, prioritize it, and zero in on the most important aspects. Acrostics feature words and phrases that serve as brain cues to help students remember information and help move it to long-term memory.

MATERIALS & PREPARATION

- Acrostic Forms reproducible (p. 133)
- 3 transparencies
- Colored pencils or markers (optional)

1. Make a list of vocabulary words from the unit of study.
2. Create an example of a name acrostic on a transparency to remind students of acrostics they

have written in the past. Or copy our example for "Kyle" (see illustration) on a transparency.

3. Write the word *biomes* vertically on a blank transparency. Make another transparency of Acrostic Forms.

Kind, caring, and funny

Yearns for new adventures and foreign places

Loyal to family and friends

Exudes energy, determination, and a desire to learn

Introducing the Activity

1. Place the name acrostic transparency on the overhead and ask, "Can you explain to me what you see and what you remember about this form of writing?"

2. Allow time for students to explain that it's a descriptive form of poetry, in this case describing an individual.

3. Remind students that if they have ever written an acrostic about themselves, they had to think deeply about who they are to create an interesting and accurate poem. Tell them that they're going to be writing acrostic poetry, but that each of their poems will be a summary of concepts they've studied, or a "sum-acrostic."

4. Show students the *biomes* transparency. Model how students could use their notes, textbooks, resource books, and other materials to find words associated with *biomes*.

5. Have students brainstorm a list of words related to *biomes*. List these words on the side of the transparency.

6. Model how a writer starts by choosing priority words that fit the letters of the target word—in this case, *biomes*—and deciding how to use other words to connect to these priority words.

7. Show students the Acrostic Forms transparency. Discuss the differences between Form A and Form B. Explain that Form A is written in complete sentences, but each sentence stands on its own. In Form B, the sentences are connected to create a complete paragraph that describes the concepts behind the word. Ask students to identify the topic sentence, supporting details, and summary sentence in Form B.

Step-by-Step Instructions

1. Write your vocabulary list on the board and ask each student to choose a word from the list for a poem. Tell students to begin reviewing their notes, textbooks, print resources, and other materials to decide on the most important information related to their words. Have them list that information and review it with the following questions in mind.

   - What information is unnecessary for a deep understanding of the word? (Cross out that information.)

   - Is there information that's redundant? (Choose well-written statements; cross out any redundant material.)

   - Which information is most important for understanding the vocabulary word? (Arrange the statements in order of importance, then replace common, overworked words with more accurate and interesting ones.)

2. Once students have identified and prioritized the most important information, have each student choose a form for his sum-acrostic (Form A or B from Acrostic Forms).

3. Encourage students to add illustrations and color to their sum-acrostics to extend their understanding of the information.

Checking for Understanding

The sum-acrostic is not meant to be assessed as a poem, unless it is part of a language arts assignment, but the content information should be assessed. Have students included accurate information? Does their work show an understanding of the most important aspects of the word as it relates to the unit of study?

Ways to Differentiate Instruction

- Have students who are learning English or who struggle with writing use Form A for their acrostic. Writing sentences that stand on their own will allow them to concentrate on the content information. In addition, encourage them to include a sketch and to add color to their work to help them remember the concepts.

- Have students who would benefit from additional processing write a brief summary of the information, in paragraph form, using the facts presented in another student's sum-acrostic.

Acrostic Forms

Form A

Biodiversity is part of every biome.

Ice can be found in a tundra biome.

Oceans are a deep and mysterious biome.

Mammals, reptiles, birds, and other animals and plants are part of every biome.

Estuaries are amazing places where fresh and salt water come together in a biome.

Similar plants and a similar climate will designate an area as a biome.

Form B

Biodiversity helps provide for basic human needs such as food, shelter, and medicines.

It comprises ecosystems that maintain oxygen in the air, enrich the soil, purify the water, and regulate the climate. Some scientists believe that the living

Organisms on our planet are only 1 percent of what has ever been on Earth.

Many species (between 50 and 200) are lost every day.

Evaluation of plants for medicines has not happened for about 90 percent of the plants we know about. Each

Species on Earth is important and has a right to continue life here on Earth.

GROUPING SUGGESTION:
independent or partners

TIME ALLOTMENT:
several days (3–4 hours)

GRADE RANGE:
4–12

Vocabulary Vellum

In olden days, people made sturdy paper called vellum from animal skins. Today there are many kinds of paper—from card stock to a beautiful yet strong type of paper also referred to as vellum, which is sometimes embossed or embroidered. For this strategy, students won't use animal skins, but they will enjoy finding interesting paper to use just for fun. Vocabulary Vellum is a creative, meaningful way to review words. Students receive a list of words that they've learned through lessons, reading, videos, the Internet, and research projects. They connect each word to their lives and choose a mini-project to represent it. The strategy is complete when each word on the list is creatively represented in a book, ready to share with peers.

Why It Works

Making meaningful connections to words is an effective memory strategy. Connections between new knowledge and past experiences happen in all kinds of ways—through direct instruction, related reading, class discussion, brainstorming, videos, and research. In this strategy, students choose how to represent and document their connections to words, then each student shares her book with a friend. Don't be surprised if you hear lots of laughter as students share the connections they made between the new words and their own lives. This can only lead to success on the end-of-unit vocabulary test!

MATERIALS & PREPARATION

- Vocabulary Vellum Project Choices reproducible (p. 138)
- Vocabulary Vellum Rubric (p. 139)
- Variety of paper
- 2 sheets of oak tag or poster board for each student
- Glue sticks
- Colored pencils or markers

1. Make copies of Vocabulary Vellum Project Choices and Vocabulary Vellum Rubric for students.

2. Create a list of vocabulary words you've taught during a unit or from a book students have read. Make copies of the list for students. (If you're using IDEA Vocabulary Log, p. 73, students should already have the words listed.)

3. Gather enough blank paper so that each student has a sheet for every word on your list. You can use construction paper, poster board, card stock, onion skin, or any other type of paper. Try to have a variety of paper in different weights, textures, and colors. (Ask parents to contribute paper for even more variety. Local businesses might donate paper that they are no longer using.)

Introducing the Activity

1. Give each student two sheets of oak tag or poster board to use as book covers. Have them start decorating the covers. Give each student a copy of Vocabulary Vellum Project Choices. Have them glue this on the inside front cover.

2. Give each student a copy of Vocabulary Vellum Rubric. Explain each section so they understand how their projects will be evaluated. Have them glue this on the inside back cover.

3. While they're working on their covers, use a random draw for students to choose their "vellum" sheets.

4. When students have chosen their paper, have them create books with the covers and sheets. Decide whether you want the books to be portrait or landscape style and how you want them to be bound—for example, stapled or three-hole punched. If you have access to a bookbinding machine, the finished books look great.

Step-by-Step Instructions

1. Give each student a copy of the vocabulary list. Have them choose a word from the list and an activity from the project choices. Tell them to write the word on the first sheet of paper and number that page "1." A student might choose the word *boycott* and the project "comic strip or cartoon." She would write the word on the page, number it, and then create a comic strip or cartoon using *boycott* in a way that connects her life with the word. She could draw a comic strip showing herself boycotting her sister's homemade cookies, for instance. Remind students to use color on every page.

2. Have students choose another word from the list and a different way to represent it. A student might choose the word *import* and create a semantic web of goods he'd like to import from other countries. Have students continue until all the words are represented in different ways.

3. Ask students to write a brief reflection on the project. Have them answer the questions below or devise your own. We have them use notebook paper for this and just slip it into their books in front of the first page.

   - Does this project represent your best efforts? Explain.

   - Which word was the most interesting? Explain.

   - Which word meaning was the most difficult to remember. Why?

4. Ask each student to share her book with a friend, who will evaluate it by completing the Vocabulary Vellum Rubric. You can also have students present their books to the class.

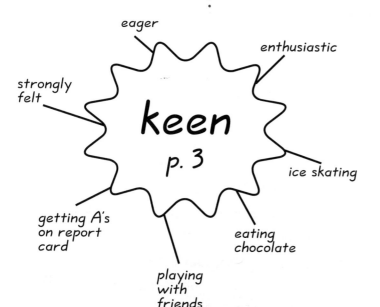

Checking for Understanding

- Students self-assess by writing their reflections on the project.
- Use the Vocabulary Vellum Rubric to assess students' books.
- Assess mastery of words using an end-of-unit or end-of-book vocabulary test.

Ways to Differentiate Instruction

- For students who are having trouble getting motivated, invite them to suggest ideas for project choices.

- Have students who are ready for more challenging work use two related words for one project on one page. Part of their job will be to figure out which words are related and to tell how they are related.

- Offer a shorter list of vocabulary words and/or project choices for students who may be overwhelmed. Assist them with their choices by helping them match words with projects that lend themselves to particular words.

Vocabulary Vellum Project Choices

Directions: Showcase your understanding of vocabulary words. Complete one project for each word. For variety, use each project only once in this assignment. Be sure to make a personal connection to each word and remember to use color.

- Word in a picture (hand-drawn or computer-generated)

- Short story

- Comic strip or cartoon

- Quotation (created by student) accompanied by illustration

- Semantic web

- Mnemonic or acrostic

- Poem

- Advertisement

- Photo with caption

- Diary or journal entry

- Simile or metaphor

- Analogy

- Fable

- Shopping list

- Horoscope

- Invitation

- Joke or riddle

- Song lyrics

- Sign

- Spooky story

- News article

- Book review

- Postcard

- Recipe

- Book title

- Dialogue between characters

- Greeting card

- 3 fact and 3 opinion statements

- Tongue twister

- Letter to a friend or someone famous

- Menu

- Interview questions and answers

- Your own creative idea (check with teacher)

Vocabulary Vellum Rubric

Name _____

Unit or Book _____   **Date** _____

Evaluator _____

Criteria	Card Stock (1): Novice	Translucent (2): Apprentice	Embossed (3): Proficient	Embroidered (4): Outstanding
1. The student's work displays understanding of the words.				
2. Personal connection with the words is evident.				
3. The work shows creativity and effort. Color is used.				
4. No project choice was repeated.				

KEY: Rate this project using the numbers below. The highest score that can be earned for any of the criteria is 4.

Card Stock (1): heavier paper, opaque; less costly than vellum

Translucent (2): a lightweight cotton vellum; moderately priced

Embossed (3): a high-quality cotton vellum; more costly

Embroidered (4): an excellent-quality cotton vellum; most expensive

What I Liked _____   Suggestions _____

Teacher Resources
Web Sites

Some of these Web sites are great for lesson ideas and others are hits with students. Since sites and content can change, we always check a site before suggesting it to students or parents.

www.allamericareads.org/pdf/wyw/ strategies/chapter/vocab.pdf
Strategies to promote vocabulary development, including use of contextual clues, idiomatic expressions, and word mapping.

www.doubletongued.org
For upper-grade students; explores slang, jargon, and new words being added to our reading and writing lexicon.

www.ed.gov/admins/lead/read/rb/ edlite-slide020.html
A summary of research-based vocabulary instruction strategies.

www.freevocabulary.com
With 5,000 words and definitions, a good study guide for SATs.

www.fun-with-words.com
Entertaining, educational wordplay, including tongue twisters, Boggle, palindromes, and hangman.

www.m-w.com
Merriam-Webster's online dictionary, thesaurus, word of the day, and more.

www.mindfun.com
A variety of games to practice words, as well as links to other sites that offer word games.

www.vocabulary.com
SAT and ACT test words for practice, links to synonym and antonym games, prefix puzzles, definition matches, crossword puzzles, and more.

www.wordexplorations.com
Latin and Greek cross-references to enhance English vocabulary skills and word studies.

www.wordphiles.info
Dedicated to clarifying word confusion; highlights good grammar usage and points out where speakers and writers fail to use standardized grammar rules.

www.wordspy.com
Explores newly coined words that appear in newspapers and magazines, on Web sites, and in other sources. This is an online word sleuth!

www.worldwidewords.org
Weirdly worded passages in the news, explanations of idioms, and interesting information about words.

http://wps.ablongman.com
Practice with context clues and word structure, plus easily confused words, dictionary exercises, and specific vocabularies for academic areas.

Bibliography

Allen, Janet. *Reading History: A Practical Guide to Improving Literacy.* New York: Oxford University Press, 2005.

———. *Words, Words, Words: Teaching Vocabulary in Grades 4–12.* New York: Stenhouse, 1999.

Baumann, J. F., E. J. Kame'enui, and G. E. Ash. "Research on Vocabulary Instruction: Voltaire Redux." In *Handbook of Research on Teaching the English Language Arts*, edited by J. Flood, D. Lapp, J. R. Squire, and J. M. Jensen, 752–85. Mahwah, NJ: Erlbaum, 2003.

Beck, Isabel, Margaret McKeown, and Linda Kucan. *Bringing Words to Life: Robust Vocabulary Instruction.* New York: Guilford Press, 2002.

Blachowicz, Camille, and Peter Fisher. *Teaching Vocabulary in All Classrooms.* Columbus, OH: Merrill Prentice Hall, 2002.

Block, Cathy Collins, and John Mangieri, eds. *The Vocabulary-Enriched Classroom: Practices for Improving the Reading Performance of All Students in Grades 3 and Up.* New York: Scholastic, 2006.

Bromley, Karen. "Nine Things Every Teacher Should Know About Words and Vocabulary Instruction." *Journal of Adolescent & Adult Literacy*, 50, no. 7 (April 2007): 28–37.

Burchers, Sam, Max Burchers, and Bryan Burchers. *Vocabulary Cartoons: Building an Educated Vocabulary with Visual Mnemonics.* Punta Gorda, FL: New Monic Books, 1998.

Chapman, Carolyn, and Rita King. *Differentiated Instructional Strategies for Reading in the Content Areas.* Thousand Oaks, CA: Corwin Press, 2003.

Gillet, Jean Wallace, Charles A. Temple, and Alan N. Crawford. *Understanding Reading Problems: Assessment and Instruction.* Boston: Allyn & Bacon, 2008.

Graves, Michael F. *The Vocabulary Book: Learning and Instruction.* New York: Teachers College Press, 2006.

Harmon, Janis M., Karen D. Wood, and Wanda B. Hedrick. *Instructional Strategies for Teaching Content Vocabulary: Grades 4–12.* Westerville, OH: National Middle School Association, 2006.

Jensen, Eric. *Teaching with the Brain in Mind*. Alexandria, VA: Association for Supervision and Curriculum Development, 2005.

Johnson, D. D. *Vocabulary in the Elementary and Middle School.* Needham Heights, MA: Allyn & Bacon, 2001.

Juel, C., and R. Deffes. "Making Words Stick." *Educational Leadership*, 61, no. 6 (March 2004): 30–34.

Karp, Karen, Todd Brown, and Linda Allen. *Feisty Females: Inspiring Girls to Think Mathematically.* Portsmouth, NH: Heinemann, 1998.

Marzano, Robert J. *Building Background Knowledge for Academic Achievement: Research on What Works in Schools.* Alexandria, VA: Association for Supervision and Curriculum Development, 2004.

Nagy, W. W. *Teaching Vocabulary to Improve Reading Comprehension*. Newark, DE: International Reading Association, 1988.

National Reading Panel. *Teaching Children to Read: An Evidence-Based Assessment of the Scientific Research Literature on Reading and Its Implications for Reading Instruction.* NIH Publication no. 00-4754. Washington, DC: National Institute of Child Health and Human Development, 2000.

Nickelsen, LeAnn. *Memorizing Strategies & Other Brain-Based Activities That Help Kids Learn, Review, and Recall.* New York: Scholastic, 2004.

———. *Quick Activities to Build a Very Voluminous Vocabulary.* New York: Scholastic, 1998.

———. *Teaching Elaboration & Word Choice*. New York: Scholastic, 2001.

Nickelsen, LeAnn, and Sarah Glasscock. *Comprehension Mini-Lessons: Sequencing & Context Clues.* New York: Scholastic, 2004.

Robb, Laura. *Teaching Reading in Social Studies, Science, and Math.* New York: Scholastic, 2003.

Sousa, David A. *How the Brain Learns*. 3rd ed. Thousand Oaks, CA: Corwin Press, 2006.

Von Hoff Johnson, Bonnie. *WordWorks: Exploring Language Play.* Golden, CO: Fulcrum, 1999.

Wood, Karen, James Harmon, and Wanda Hedrick. "Recommendations from Research for Teaching Vocabulary to Diverse Learners." *Middle School Journal*, 35, no. 5 (May 2004): 57–63.

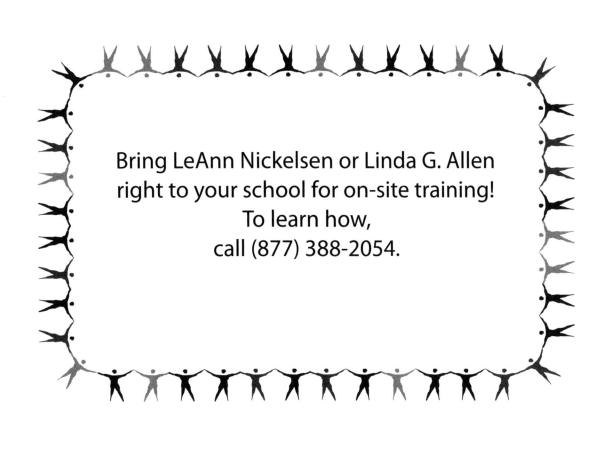

Bring LeAnn Nickelsen or Linda G. Allen
right to your school for on-site training!
To learn how,
call (877) 388-2054.